BEAUTIFUL MUSIC

COLORING BOOK

BY HAFAPEA

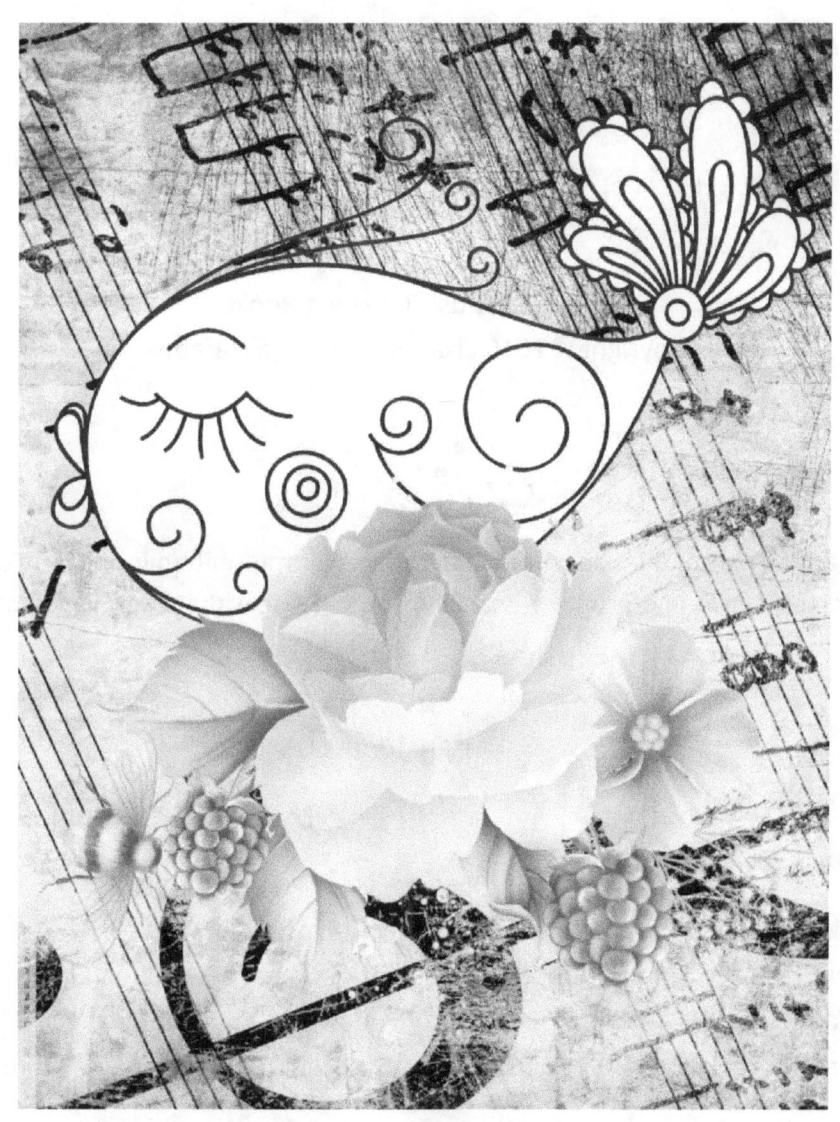

60 MUSICALLY FLORAL BIRD IMAGES FOR YOU TO COLOR

COLOR TO THE RHYTHM OF YOUR HEART.

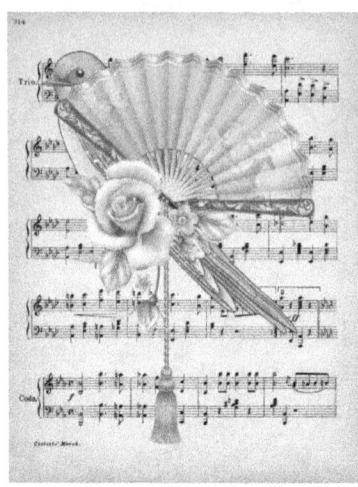

Beautiful Music Coloring Book
Copyright ©2016 Lisa Mayette, aka Hafapea

ISBN-13: 9781533164001
ISBN-10: 1533164002

Other titles available include:

- Persnickety Patterns Coloring Book: A collection of 60 fun patterns
- Flaming Fractals Coloring Book: A collection of 60 gray scale fractal art images
- Synecdotal Synergy Coloring Book: A collection of 60 uplifting images
- Mesmerizing Metaphor Coloring Book s: A collection of 60 black & white kaleidoscope images
- Floral Fancies Coloring Book Journal: A collection of 60 gray scale flower bouquets on black & white kaleidoscope backgrounds with space for writing underneath.

314

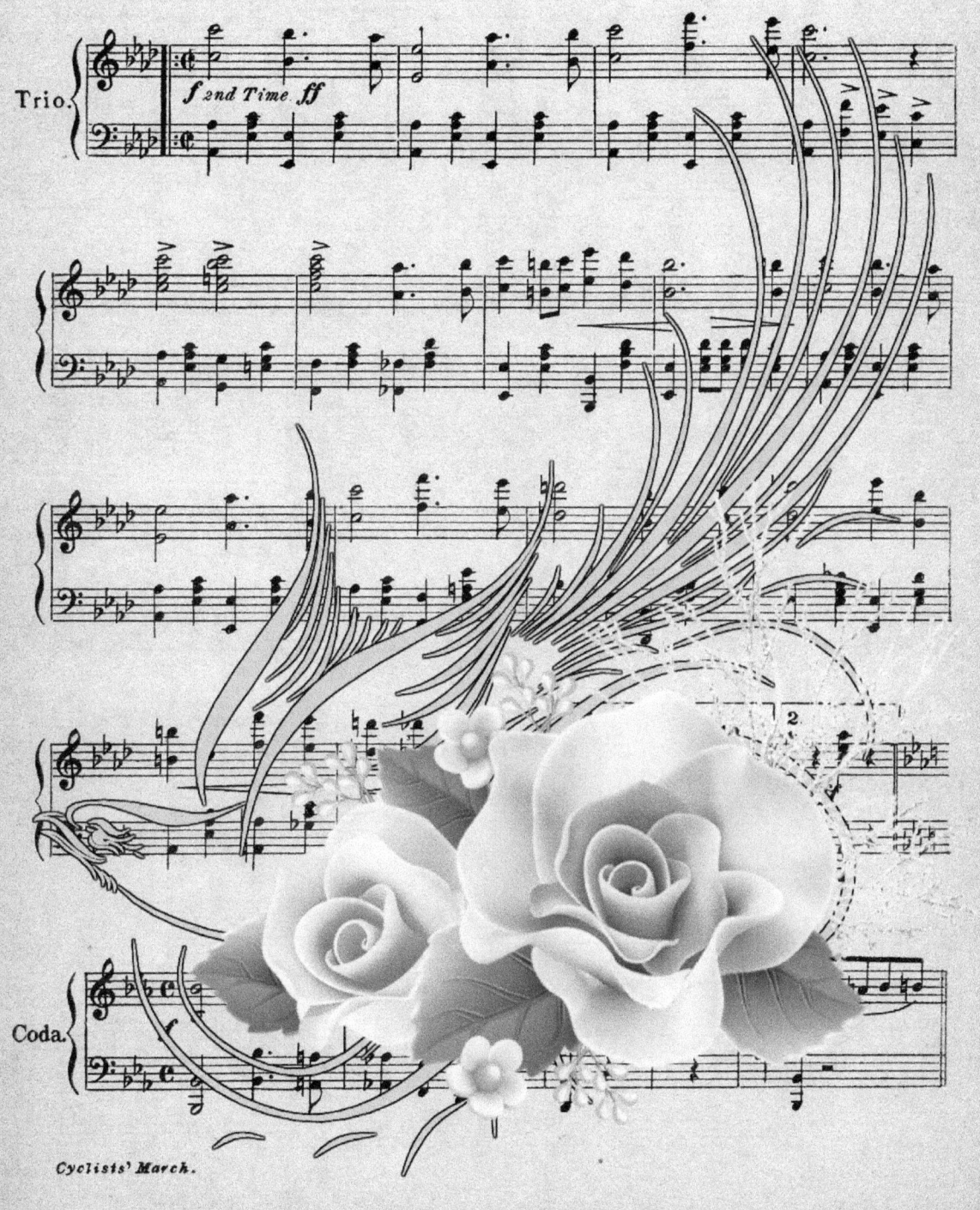

Trio.

f 2nd Time ff

Coda.

Cyclists' March.

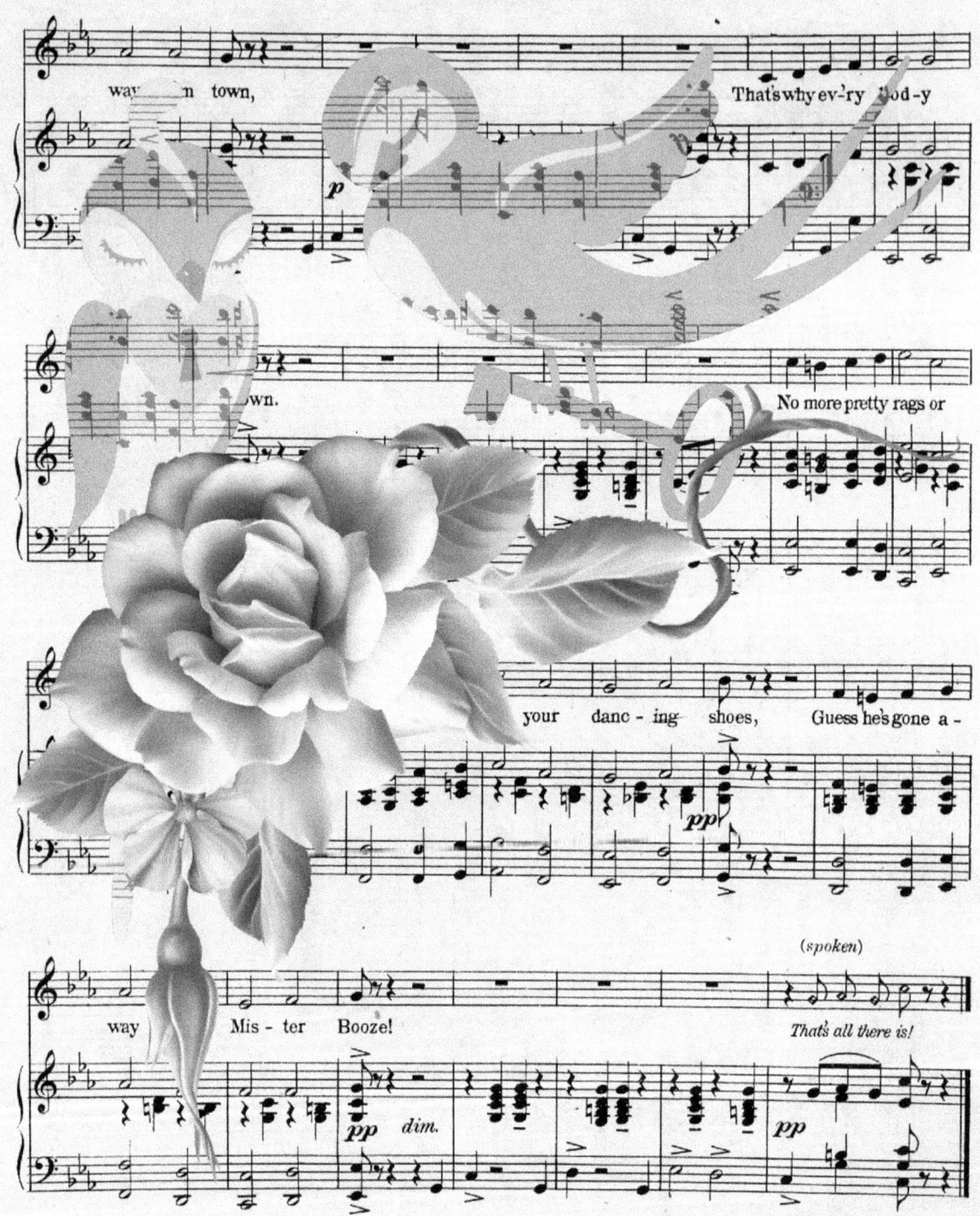

way in town,   That's why ev'ry bod-y

p

own.   No more pretty rags or

your   danc - ing   shoes,   Guess he's gone a -

pp

(spoken)

way   Mis - ter   Booze!   *That's all there is!*

pp dim.   pp

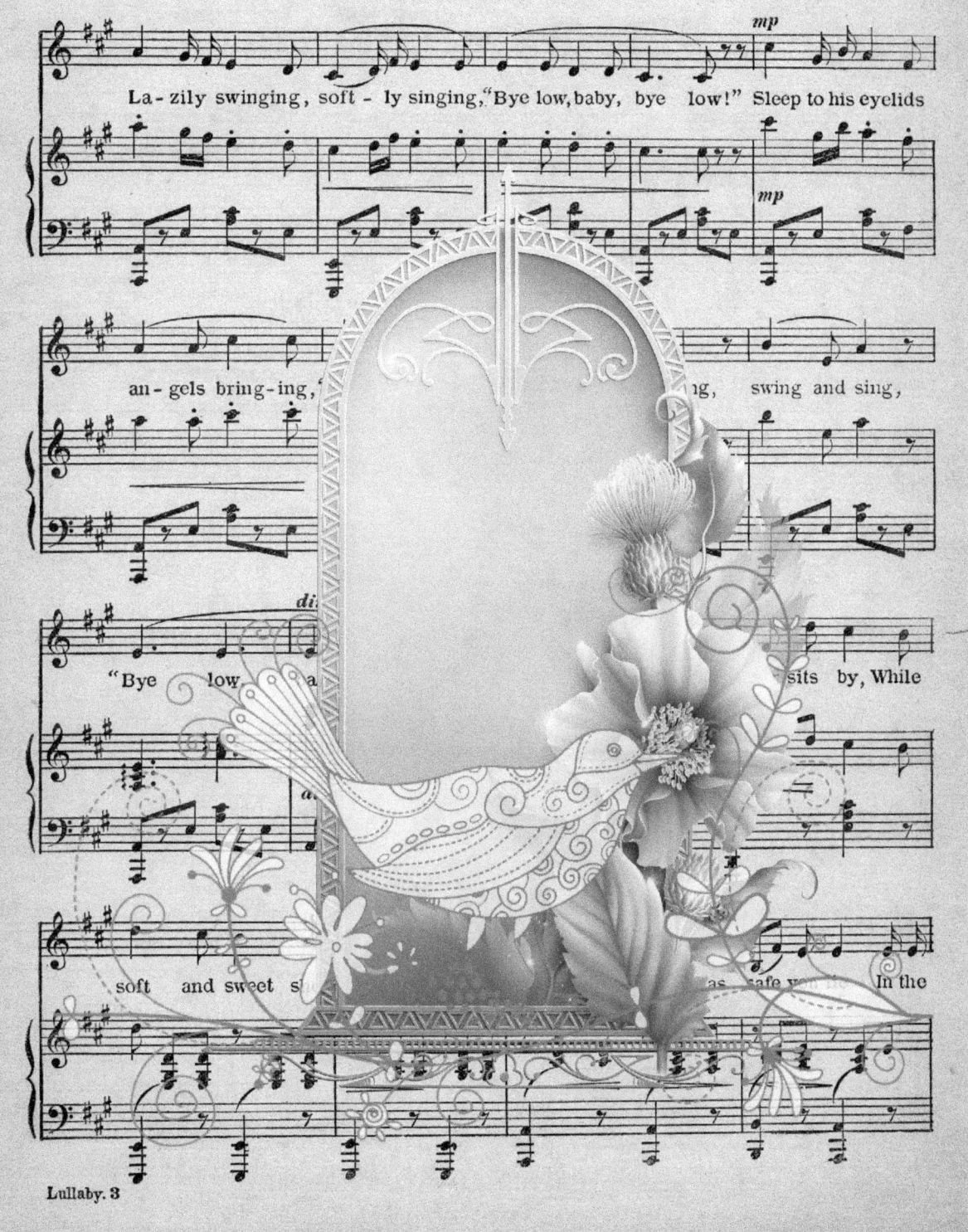

La - zily swinging, soft - ly singing, "Bye low, baby, bye low!" Sleep to his eyelids

an - gels bring-ing, ng, swing and sing,

"Bye low a sits by, While

soft and sweet s as afe In the

Lullaby. 3

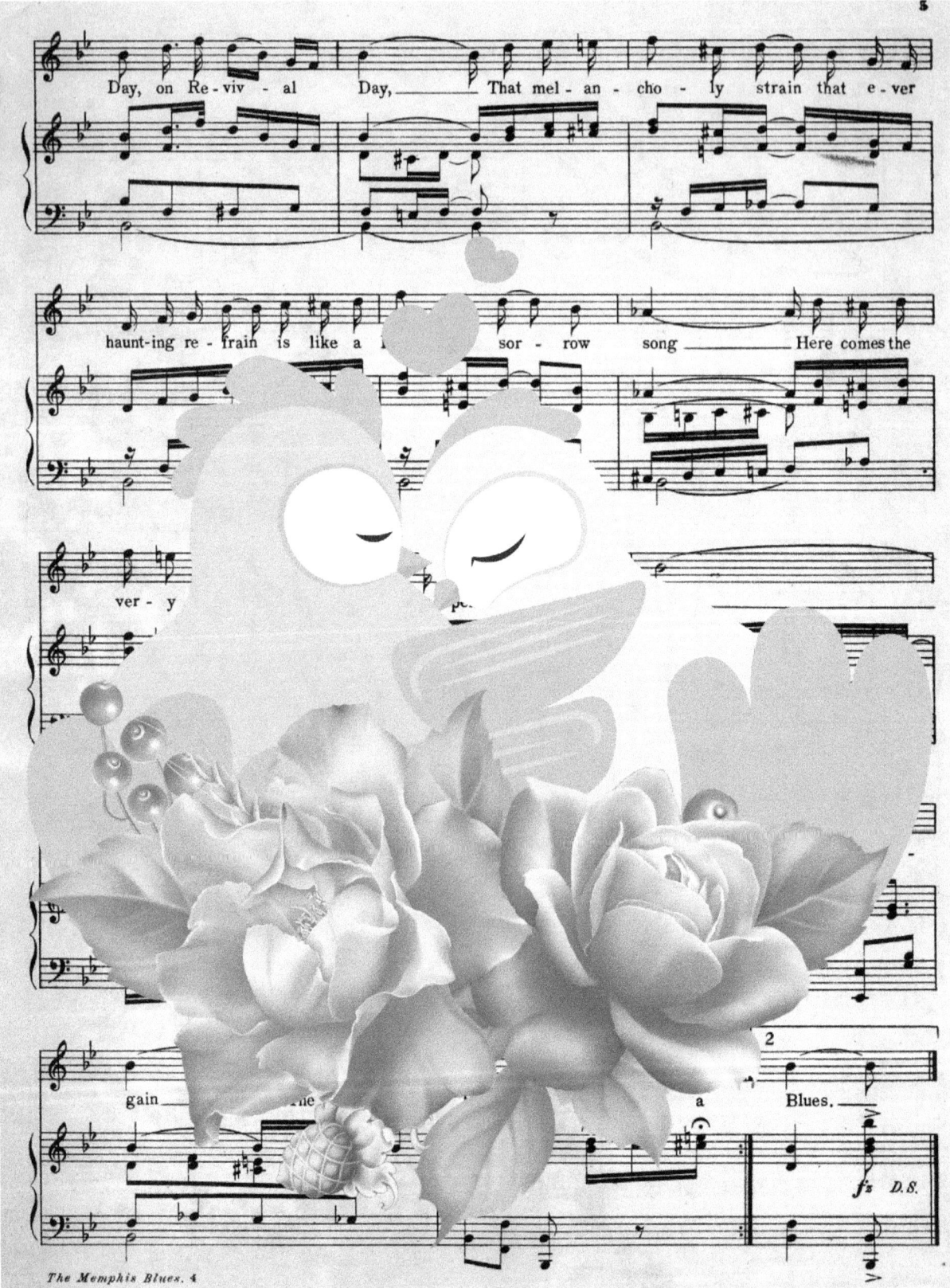

Day, on Re - viv - al Day, _____ That mel - an - cho - ly strain that e - ver

haunt-ing re - frain is like a _____ sor - row song _____ Here comes the

ver - y

gain _____ _____ a Blues. _____

fz D.S.

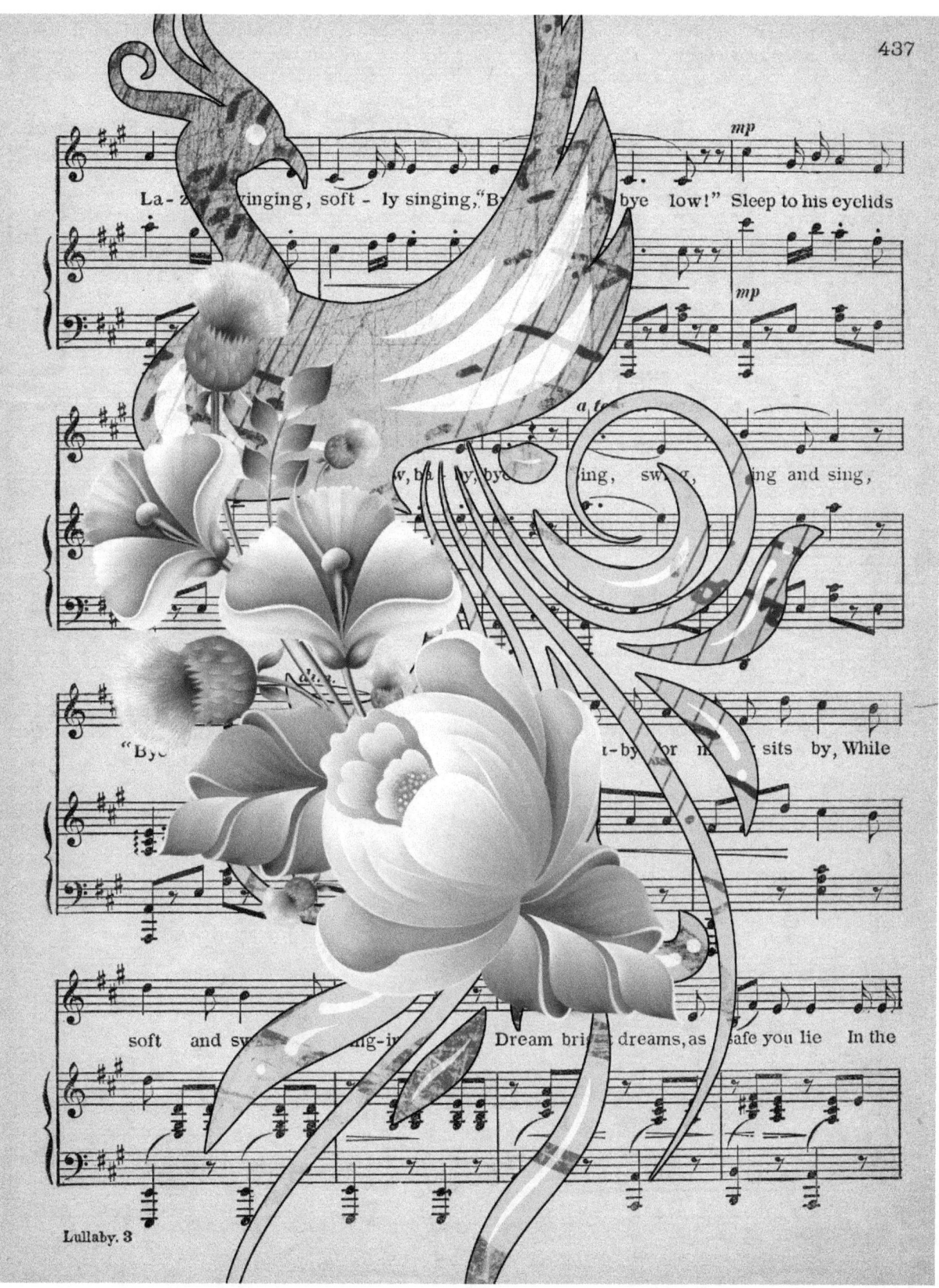

La-z... inging, soft - ly singing,"B... bye low!" Sleep to his eyelids

mp

mp

a te

...w, ba... by, bye... ing, swi...g, ...ing and sing,

"By... ...t-by ...or ...r sits by, While

soft and sw... ...ng-i... Dream bri... dreams, as ...afe you lie In the

Lullaby. 3

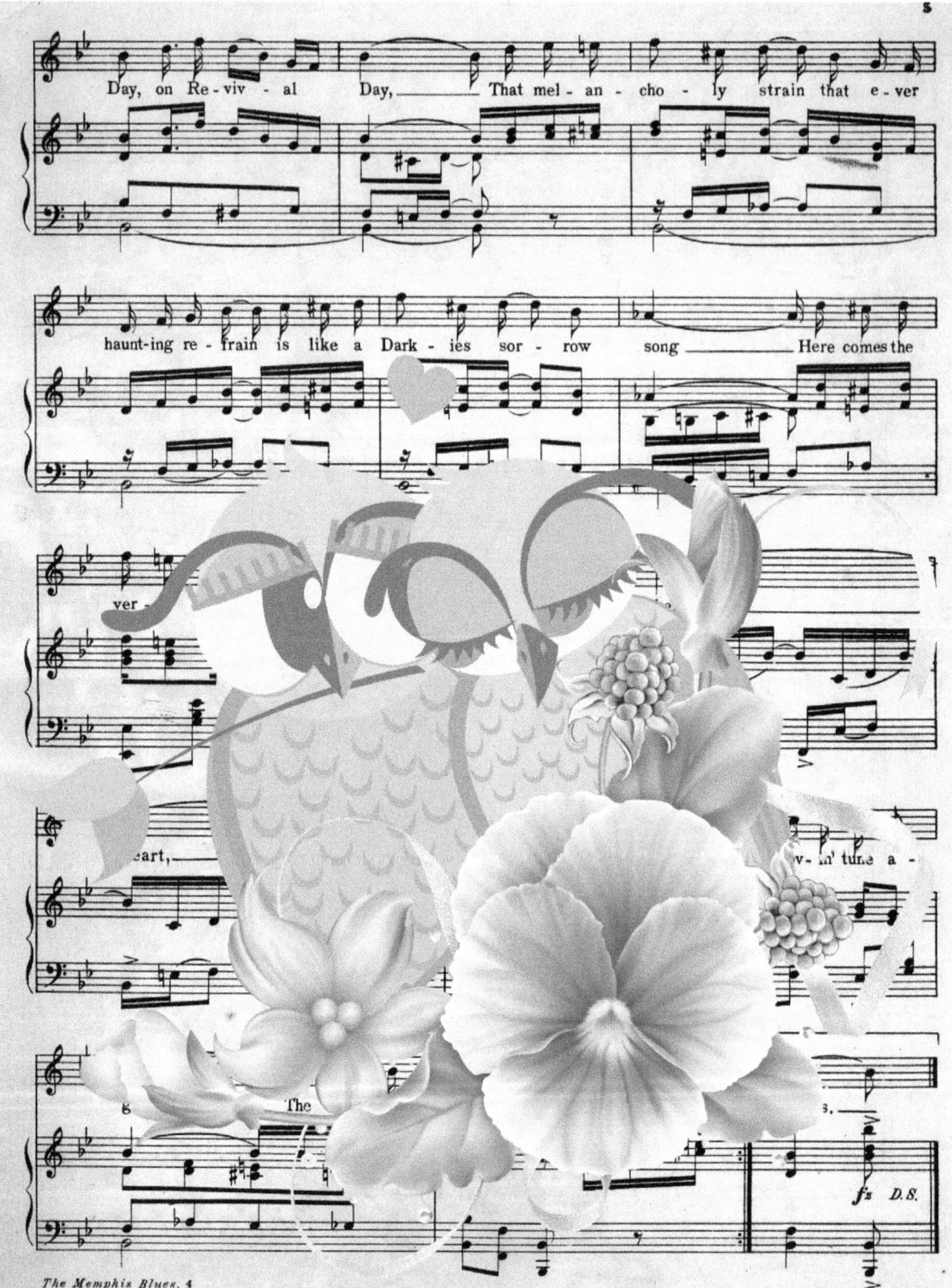

Day, on Re - viv - al Day, _____ That mel - an - cho - ly strain that e - ver

haunt-ing re - frain is like a Dark - ies sor - row song _____ Here comes the

ver-

eart,

g

The

s,

fz D.S.

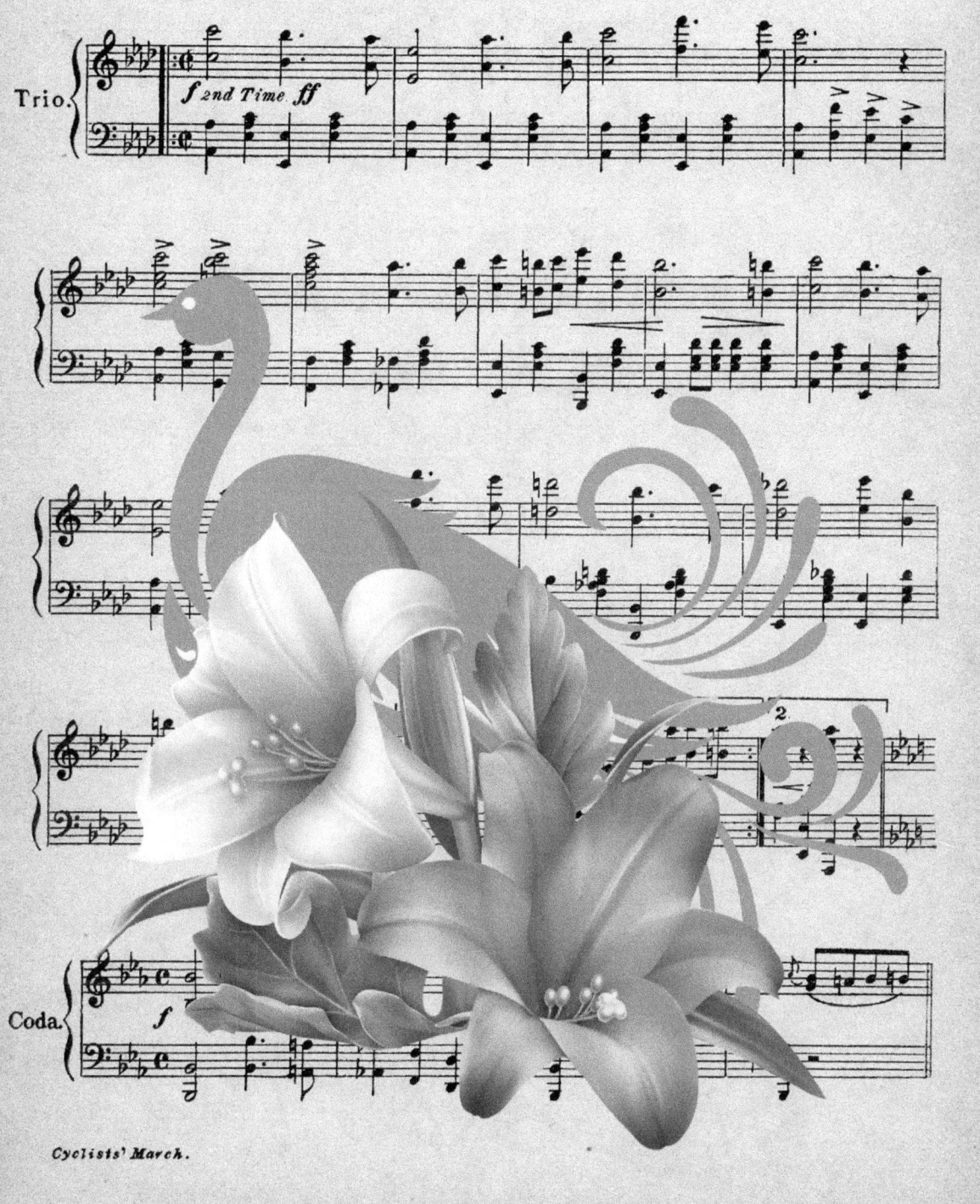

Trio.

f *2nd Time* *ff*

Coda. *f*

Cyclists' March.

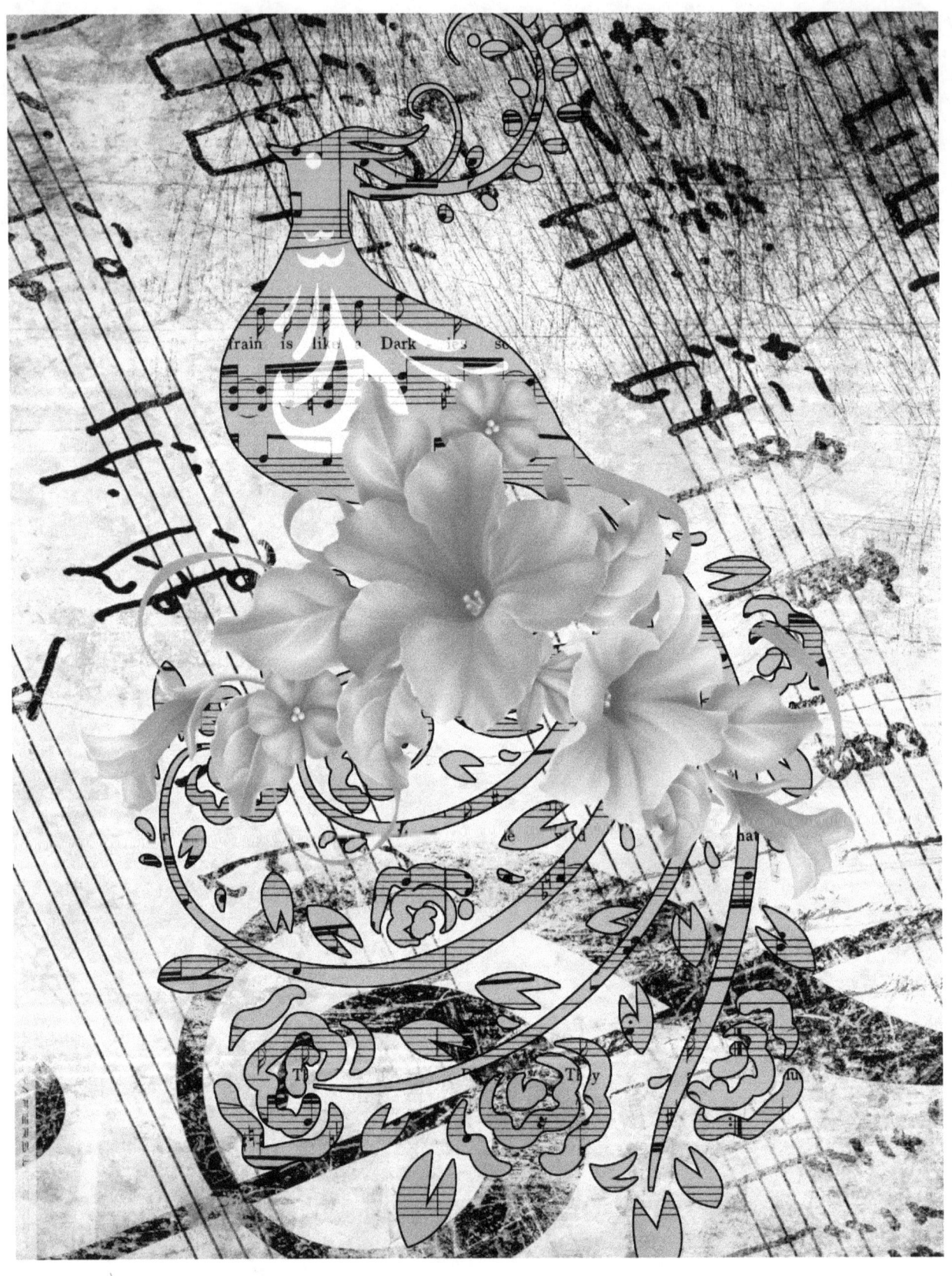

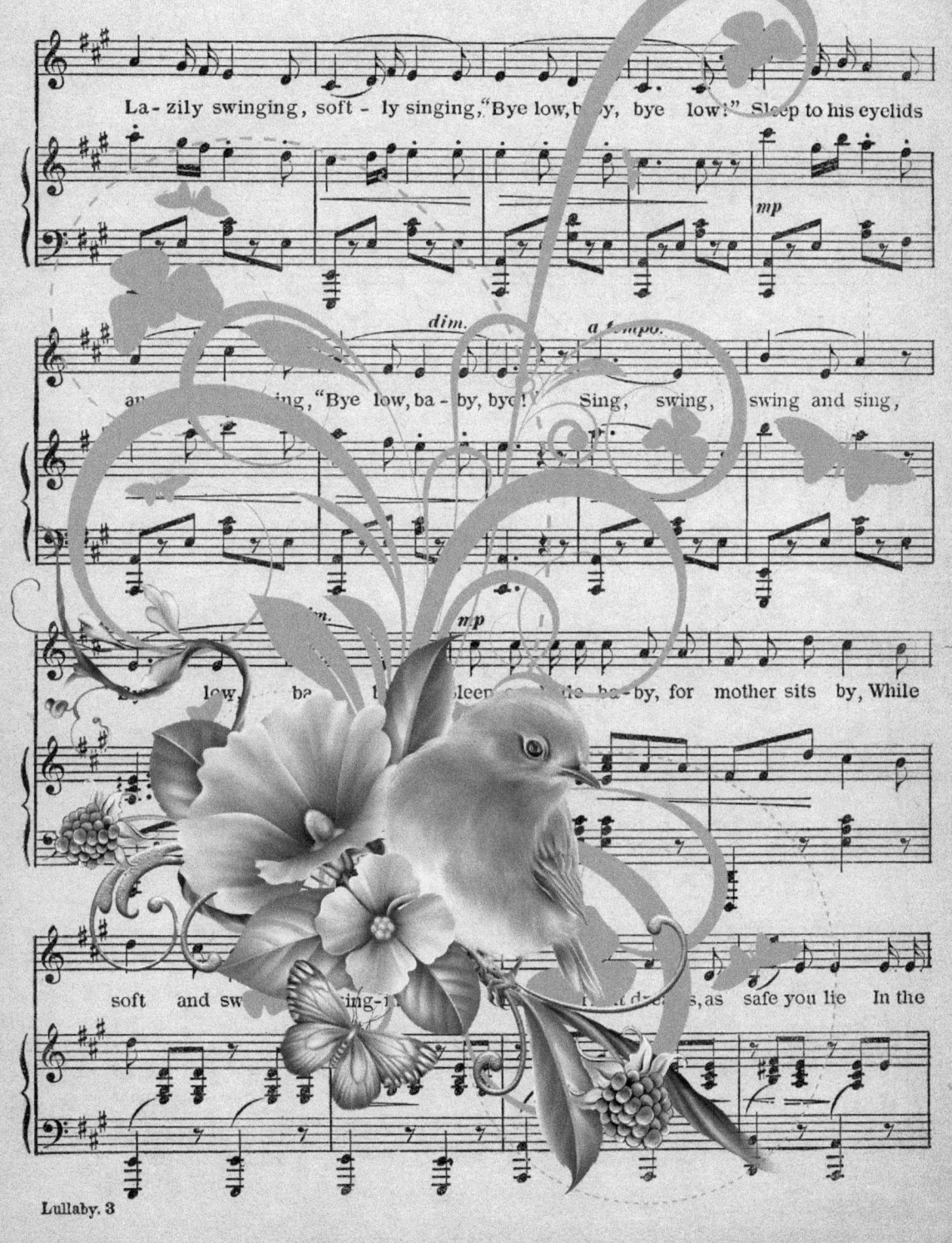

La - zily swinging, soft - ly singing, "Bye low, baby, bye low!" Sleep to his eyelids

dim. *a tempo.*

and singing, "Bye low, ba - by, bye!" Sing, swing, swing and sing,

mp

low, ba - by, Sleep little ba - by, for mother sits by, While

soft and sweet singing-time dreams, as safe you lie In the

Lullaby. 3

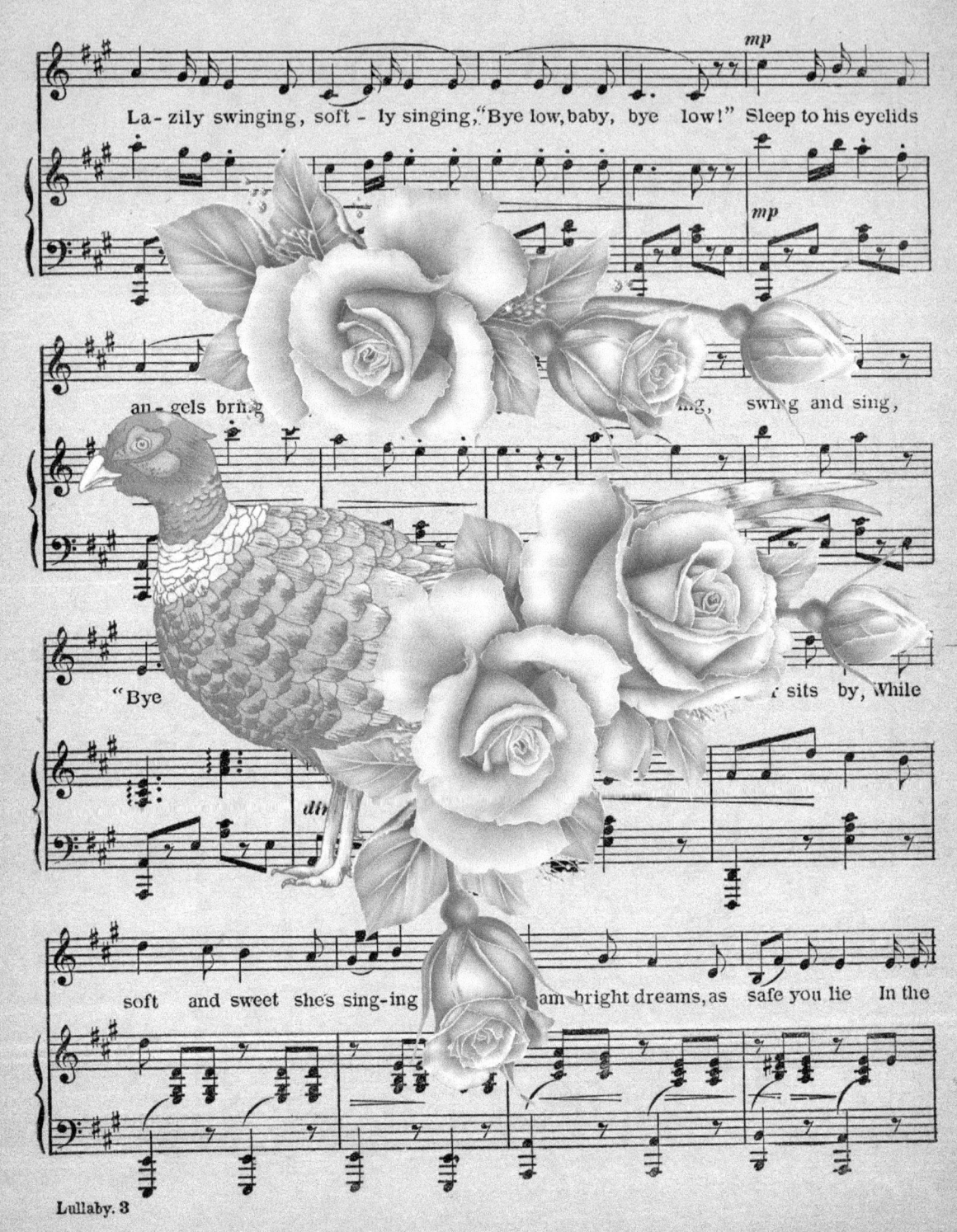

Lullaby. 3

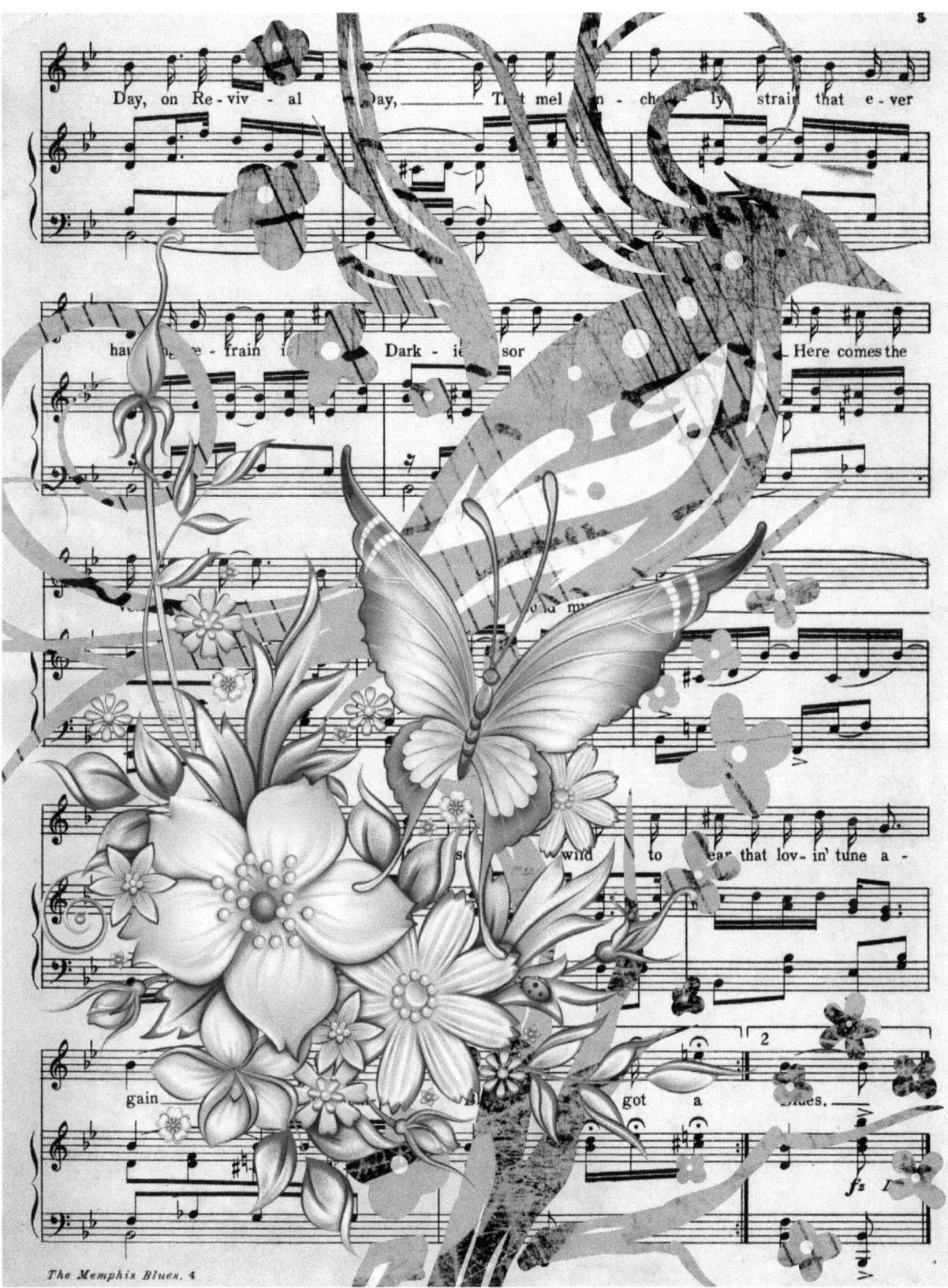

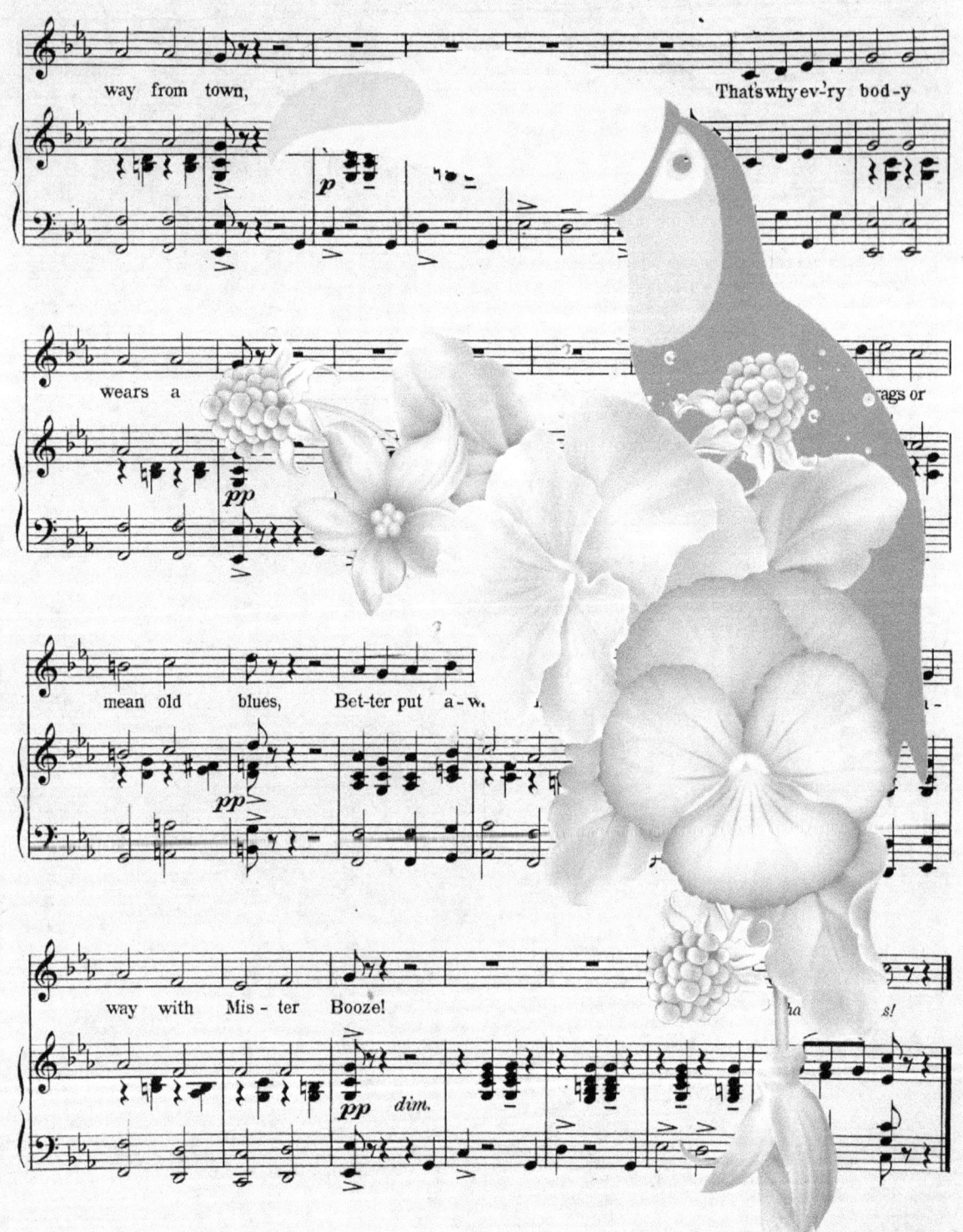

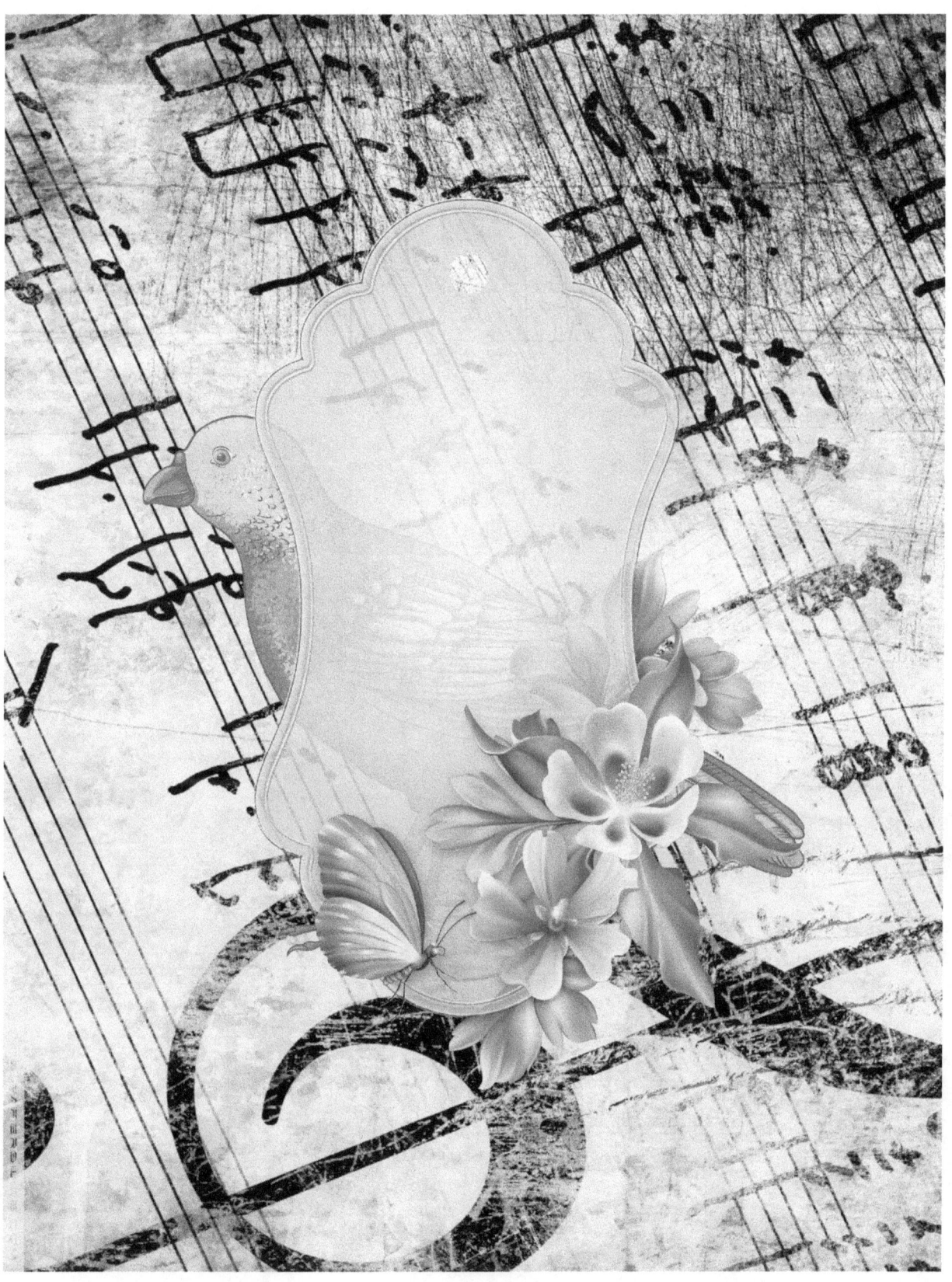

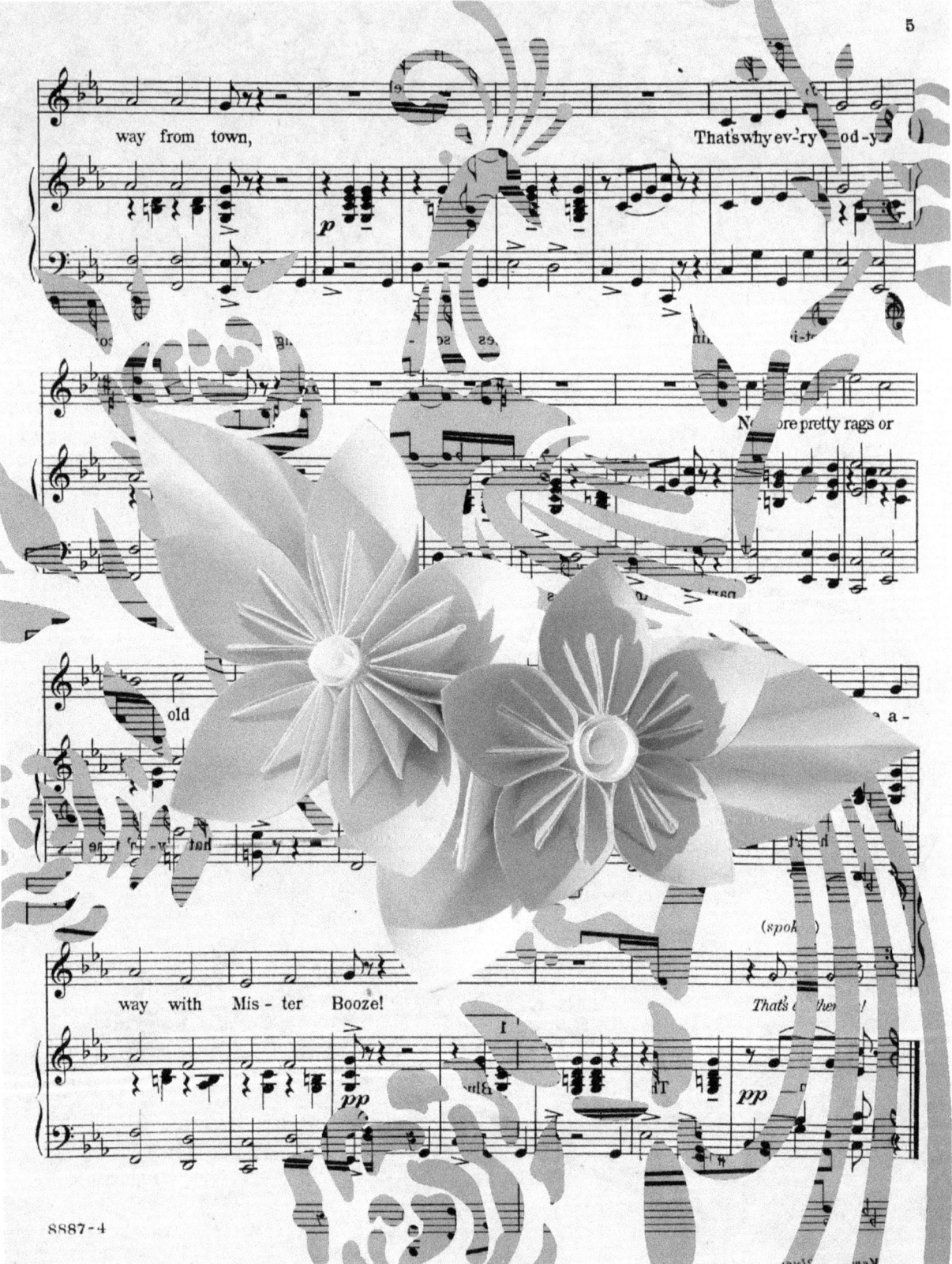

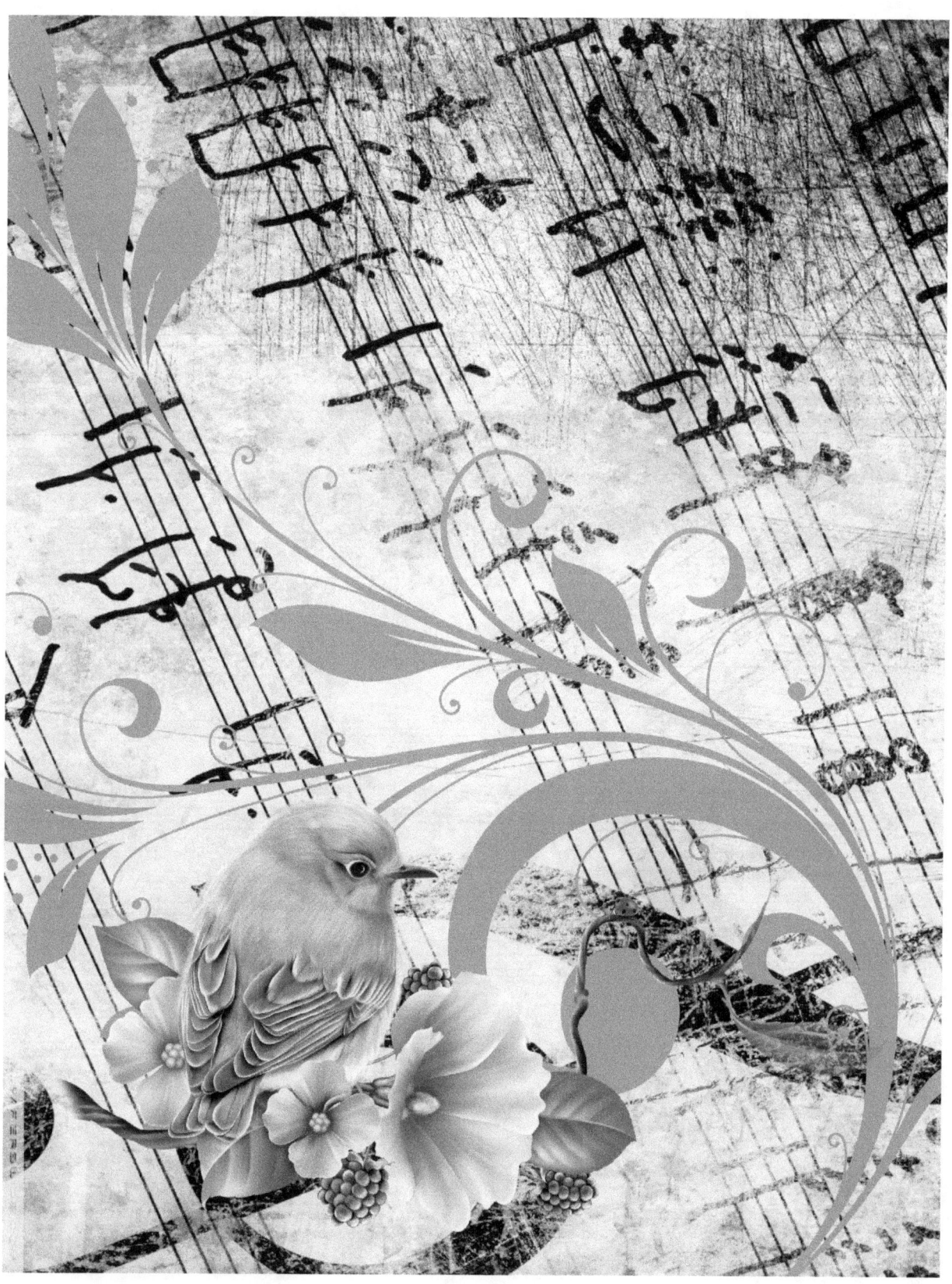

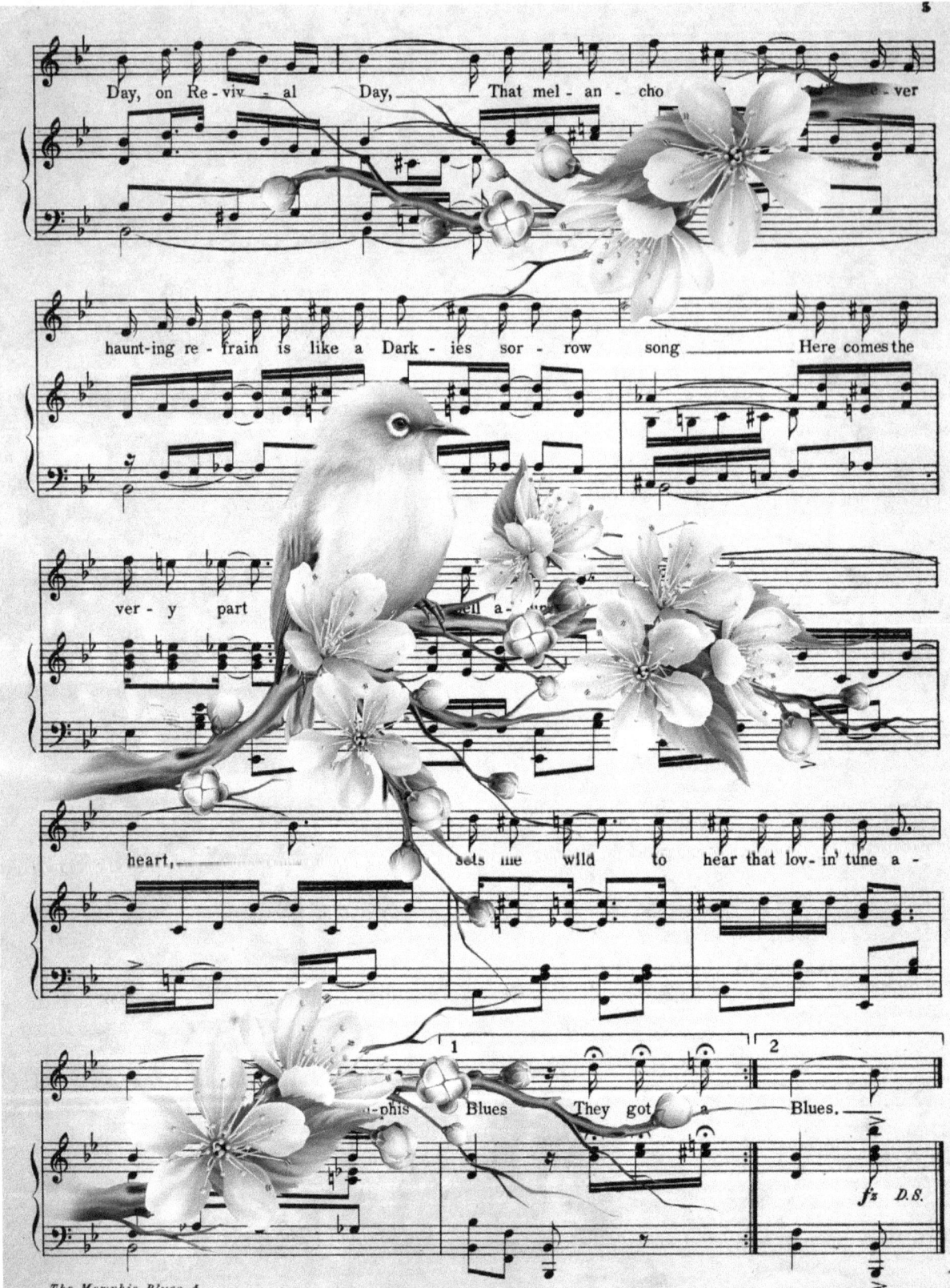

Day, on Re - viv - al Day, That mel - an - cho - - - ver

haunt-ing re - frain is like a Dark - ies sor - row song _____ Here comes the

ver - y part _____ sets me wild to hear that lov- in' tune a -

-phis Blues They got a Blues.

fz D.S.

The Memphis Blues. 4

314

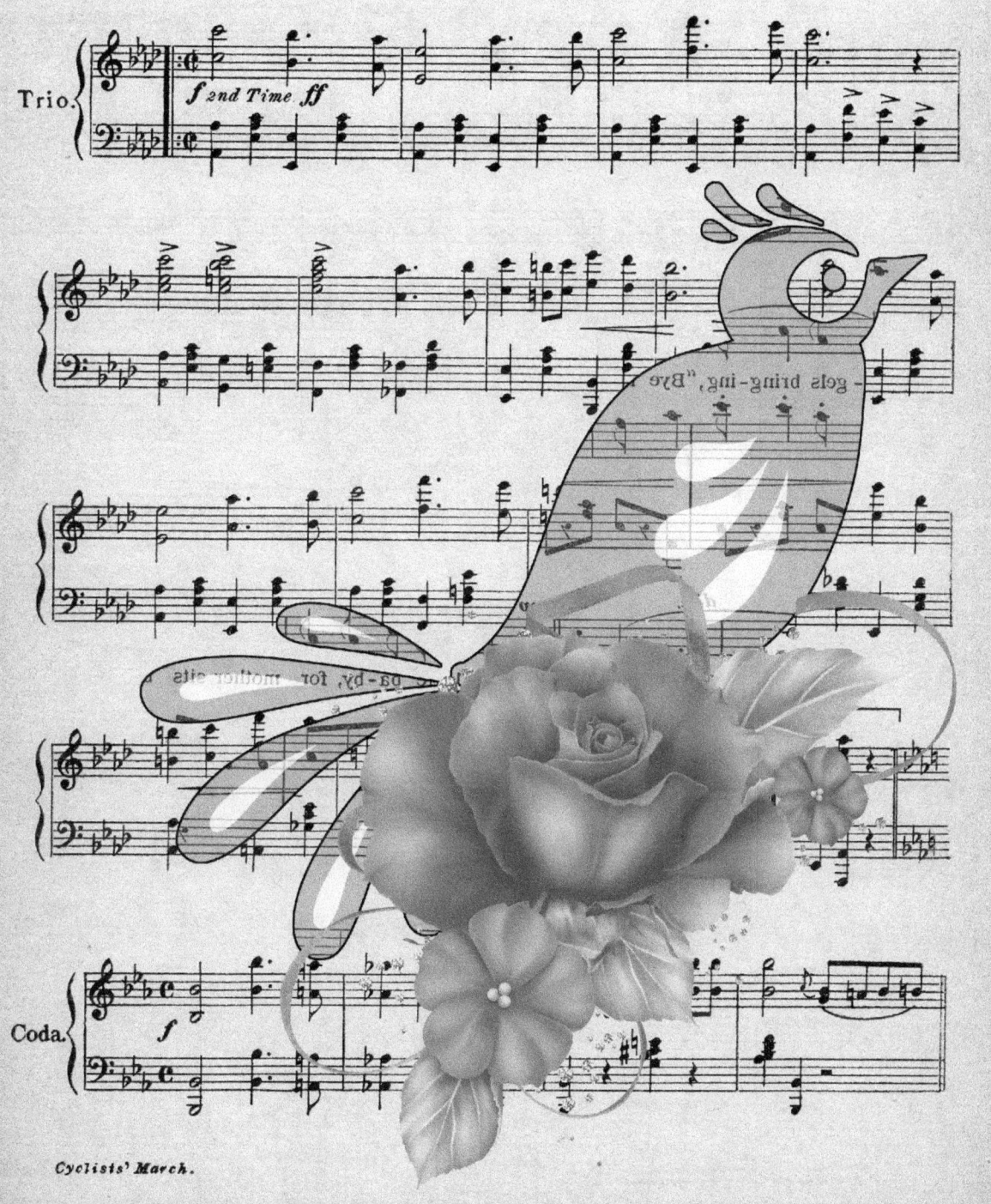

Trio.

f 2nd Time *ff*

Coda.

f

Cyclists' March.

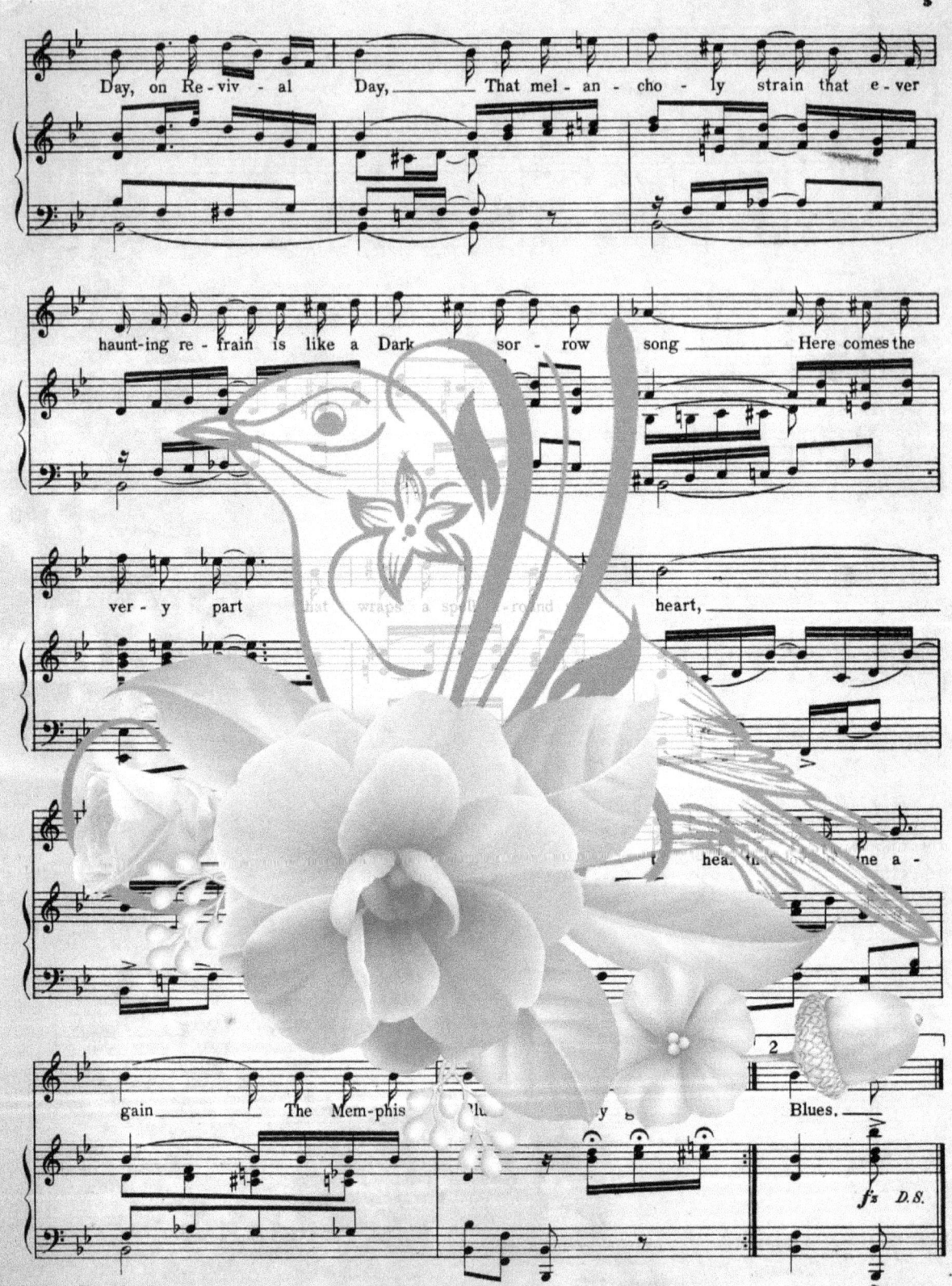

Day, on Re - viv - al Day, _____ That mel - an - cho - ly strain that e - ver

haunt-ing re - frain is like a Dark sor - row song _____ Here comes the

ver - y part that wraps a spell a - round heart, _____

hea. the whine a - gain _____ The Mem-phis Blues.

Blues.

2

fs   D.S.

The Memphis Blues. 4

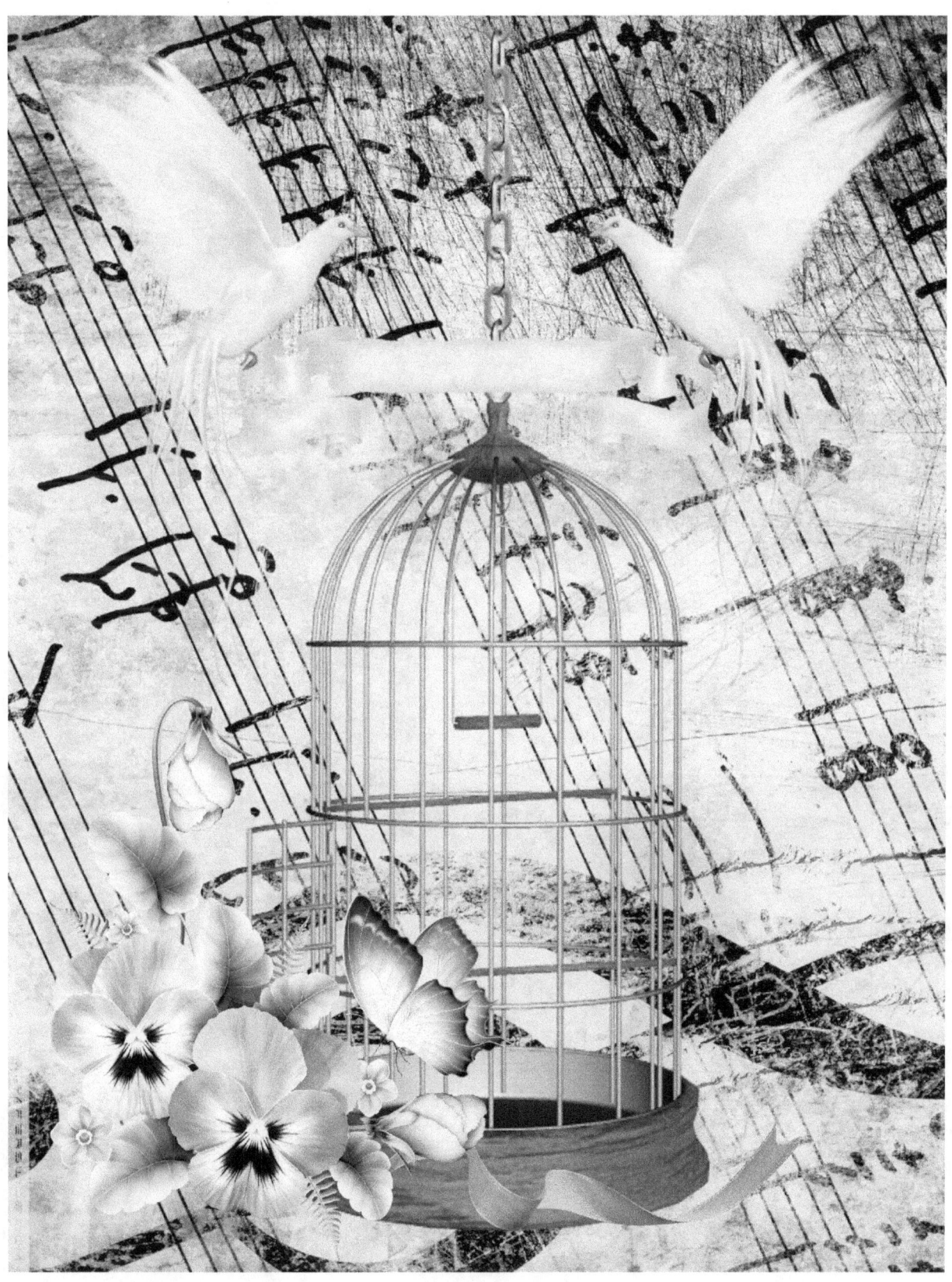

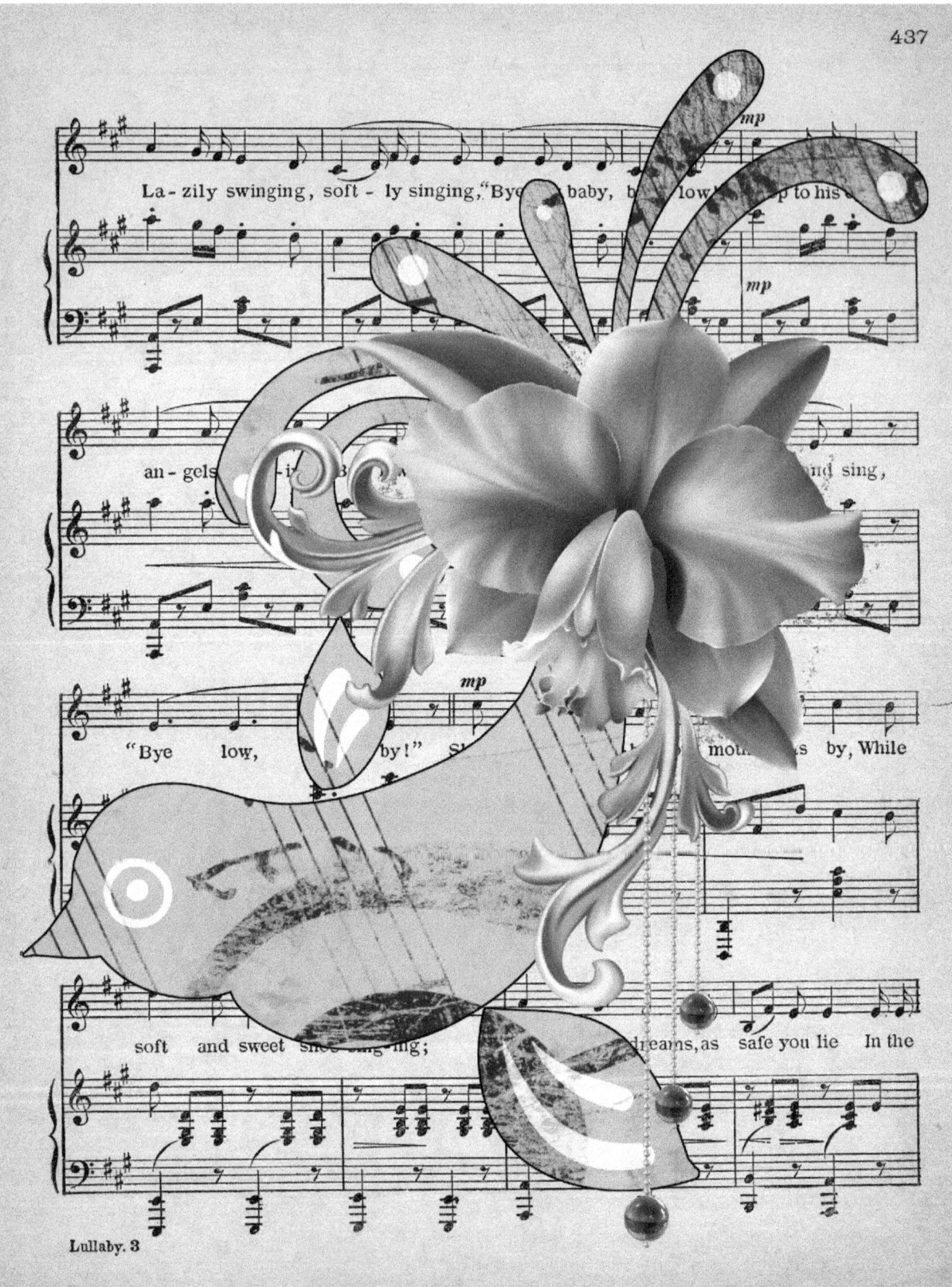

5

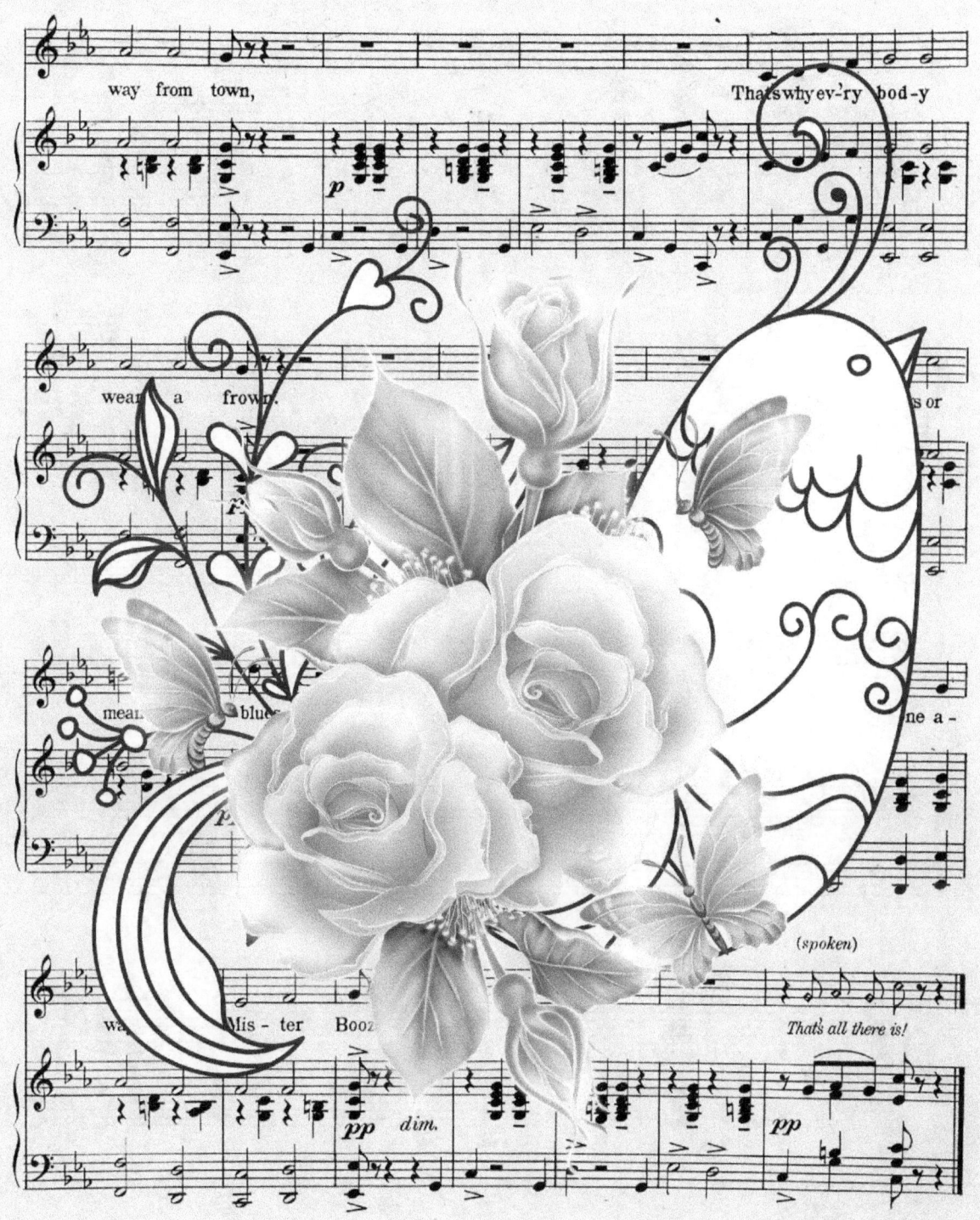

way from town,

Thatswhyev'ry bod-y

wear a frown.

s or

mean blue

ne a-

(spoken)

That's all there is!

wa Mis-ter Booz

p

pp dim.

pp

8887-4

314

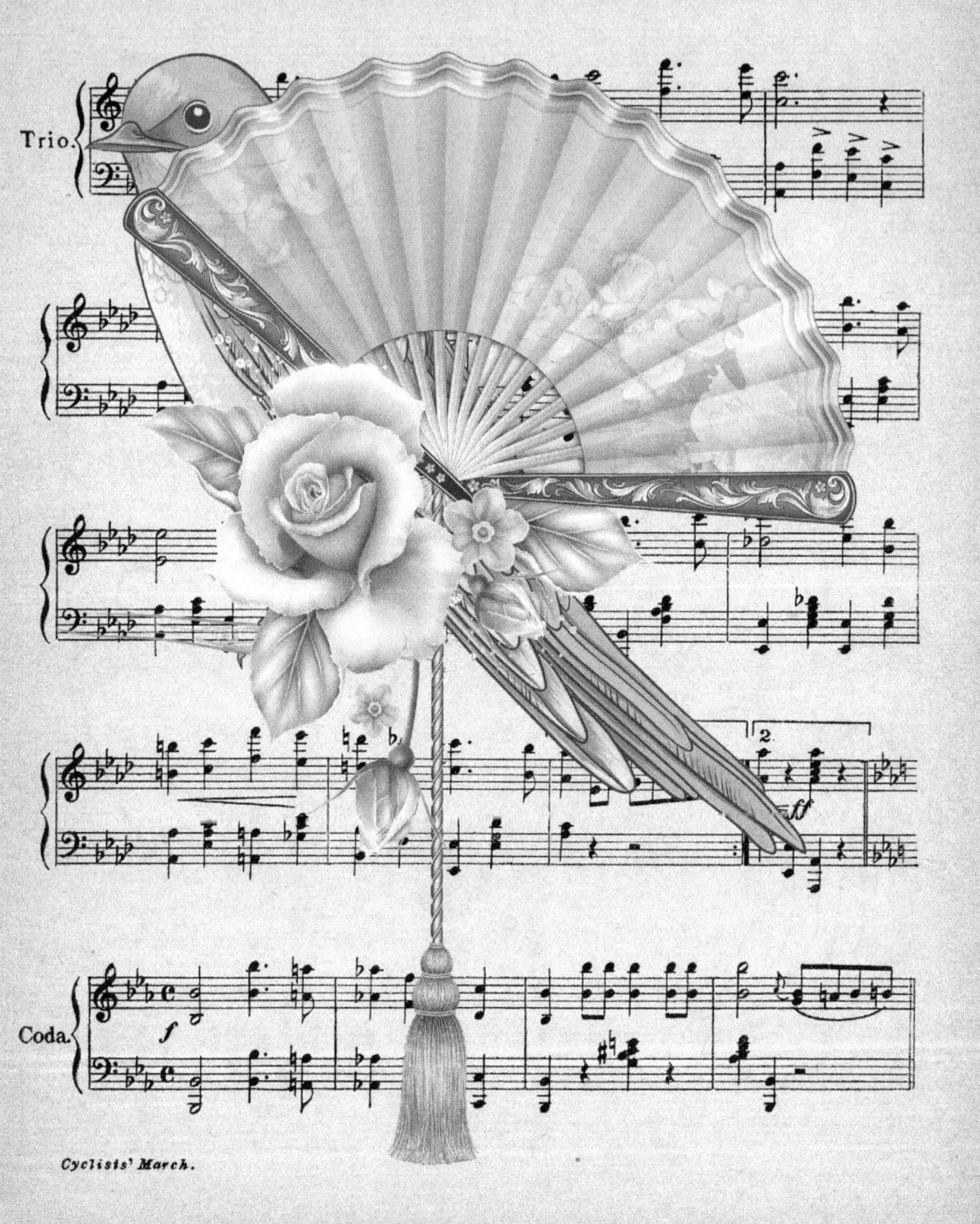

Trio.

Coda.

Cyclists' March.

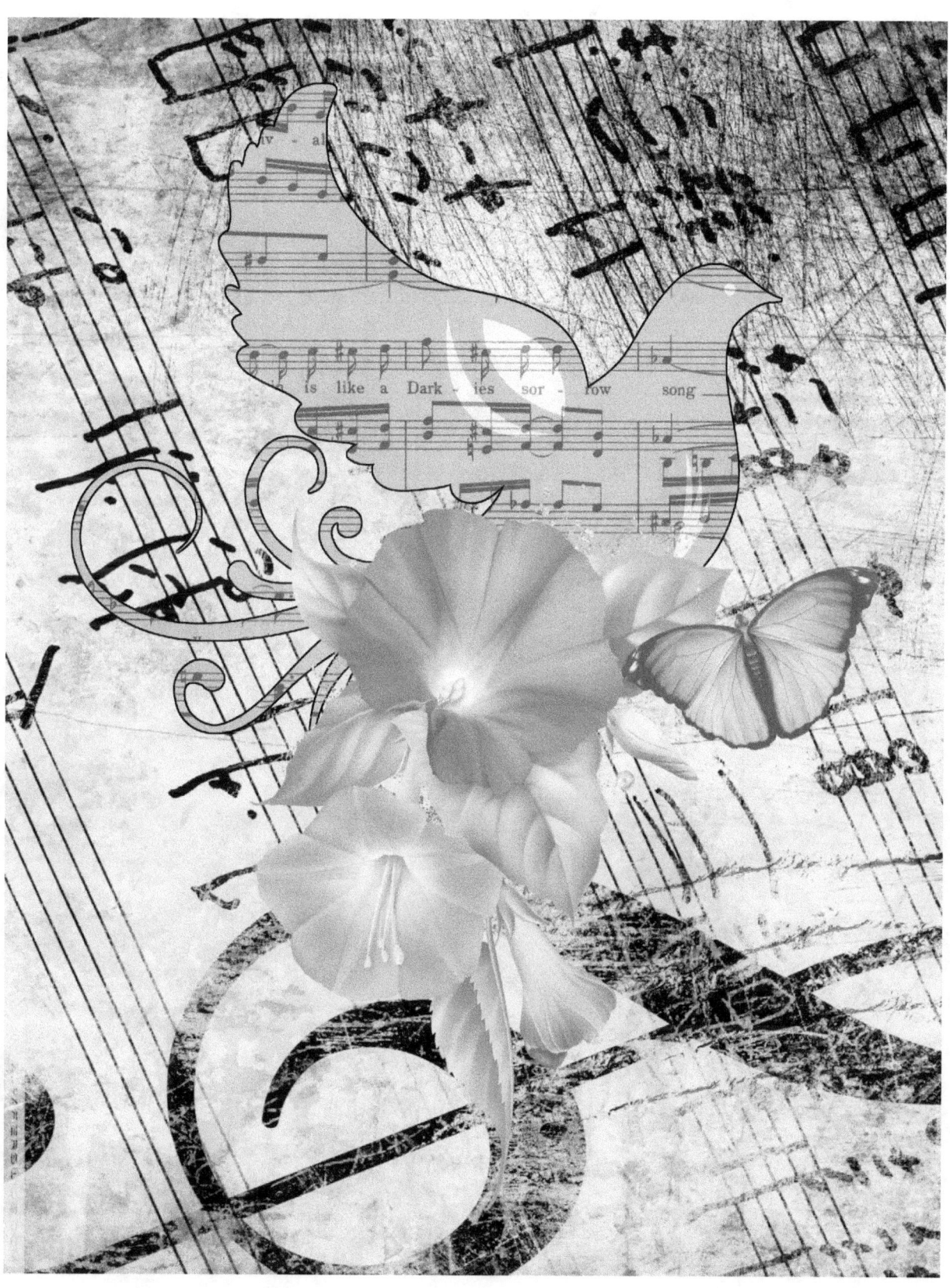

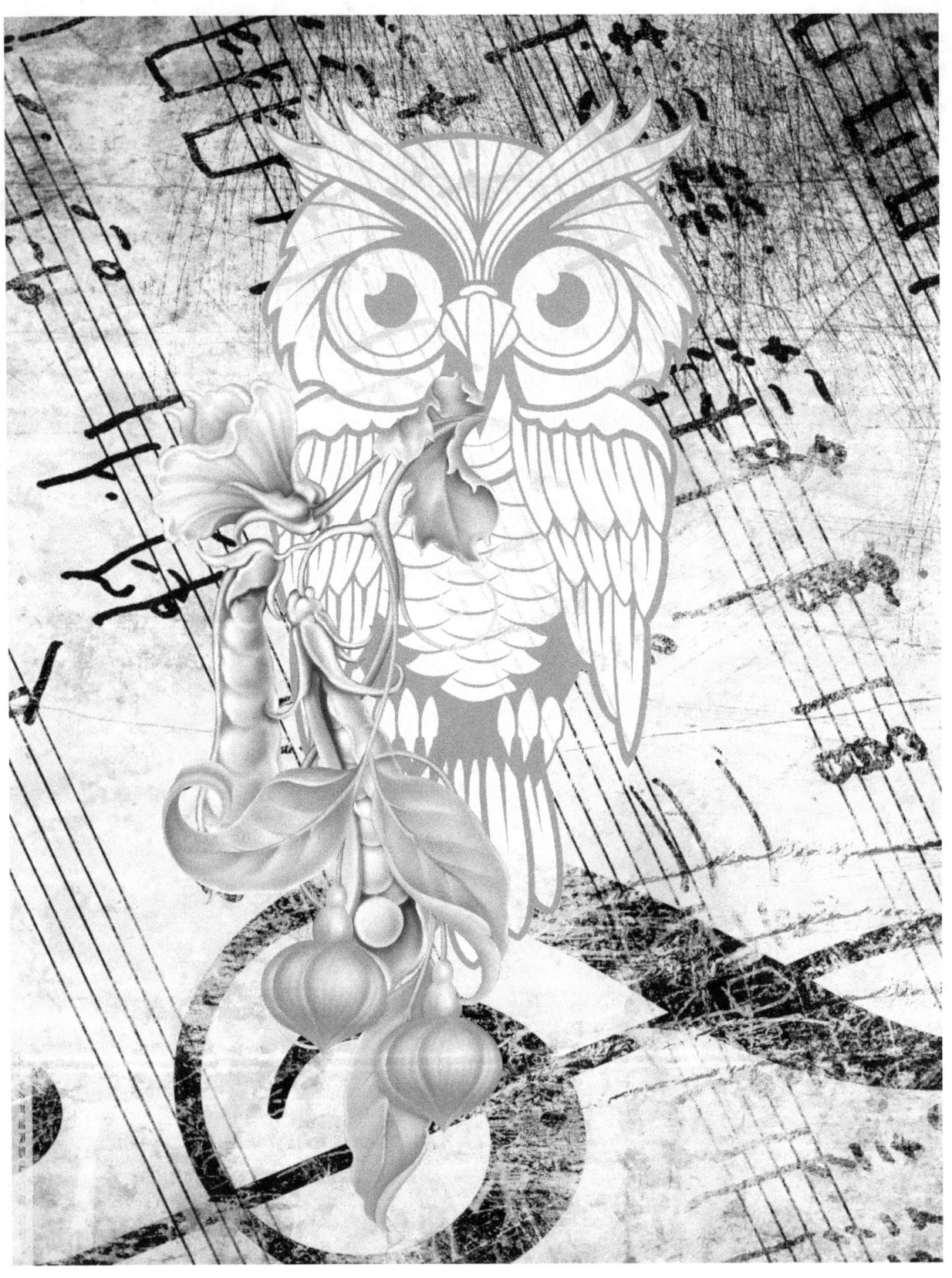

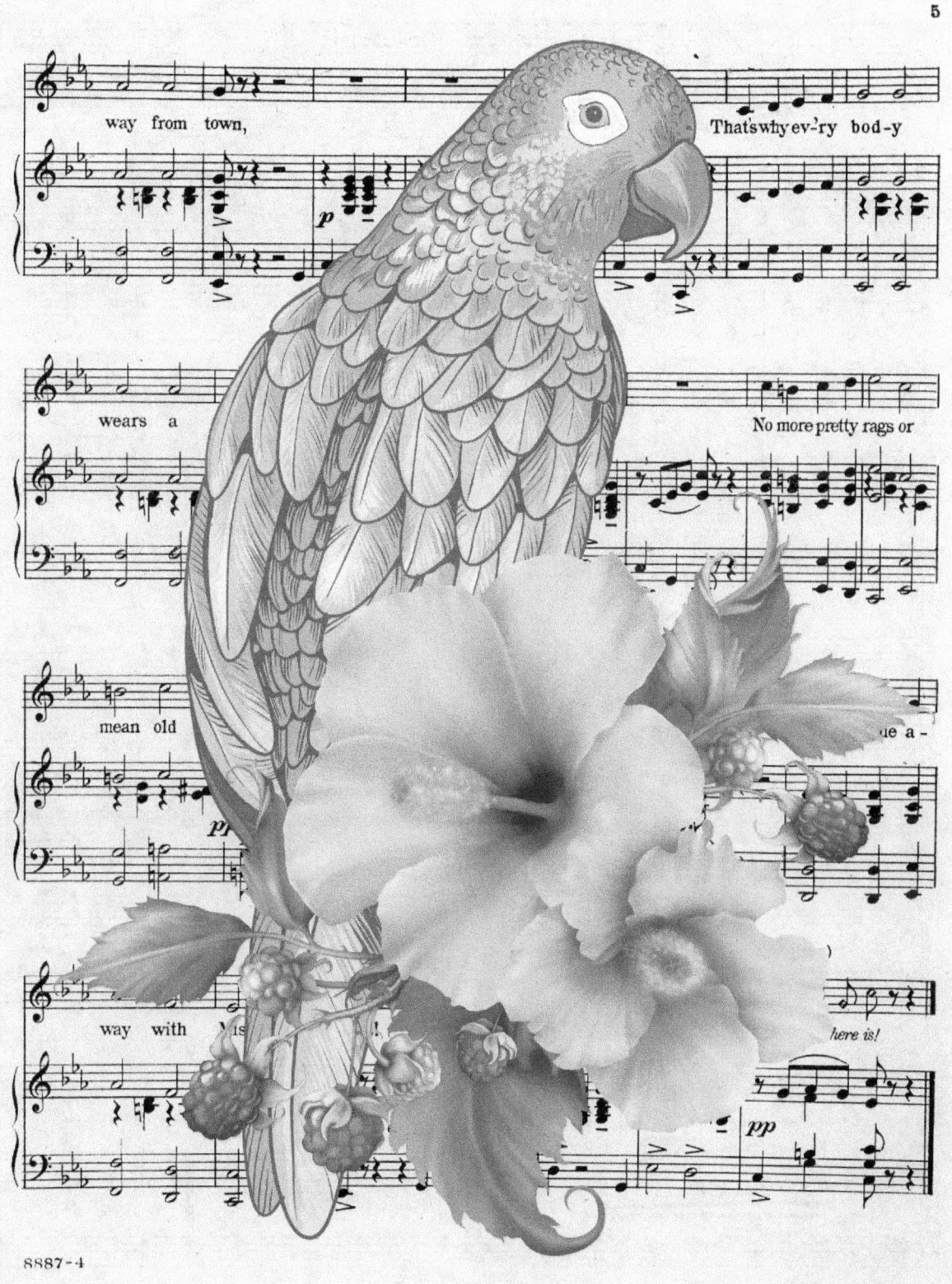

way from town,

That's why ev'ry bod-y

wears a

No more pretty rags or

mean old

ue a-

way with M   !

here is!

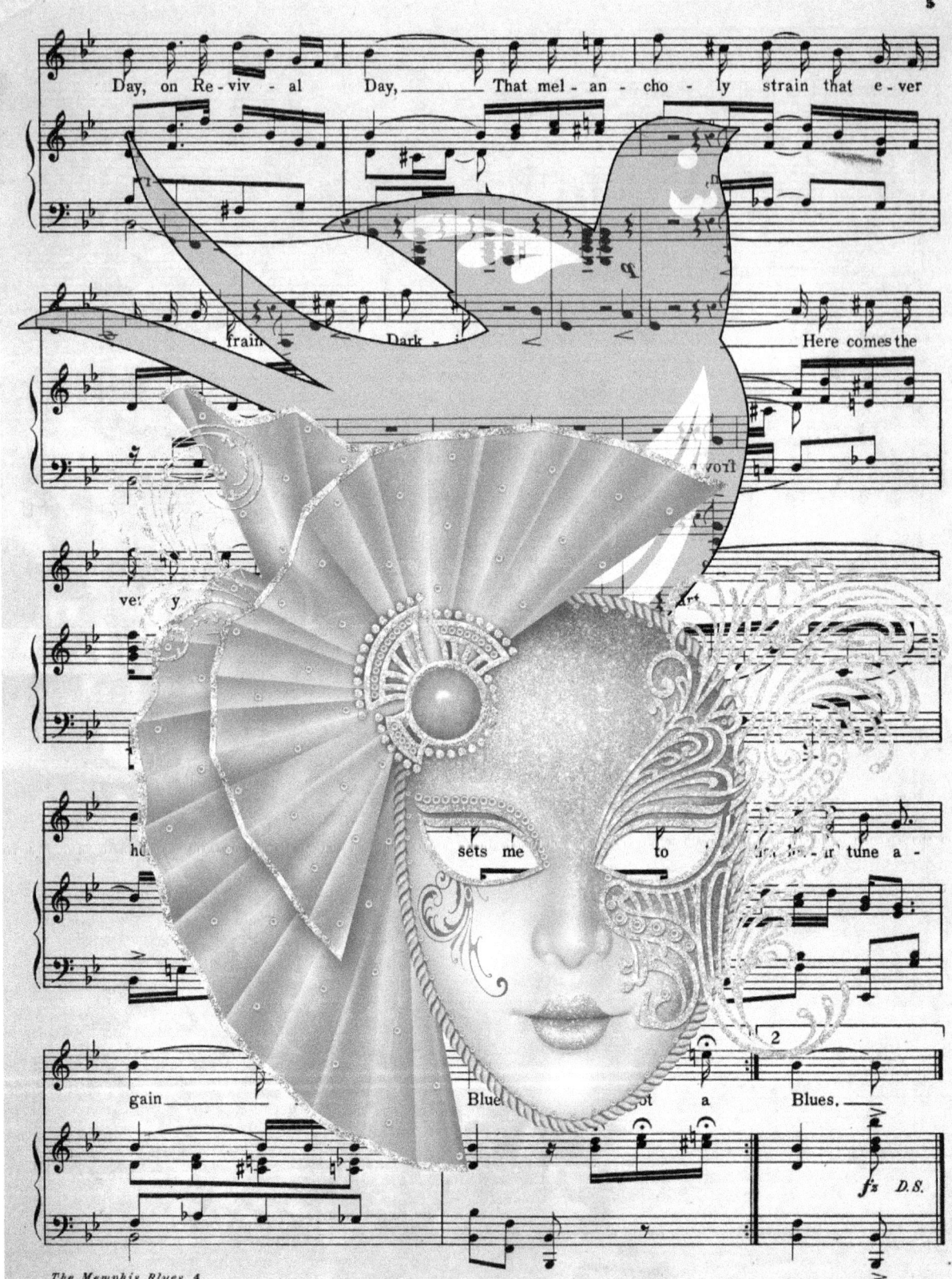

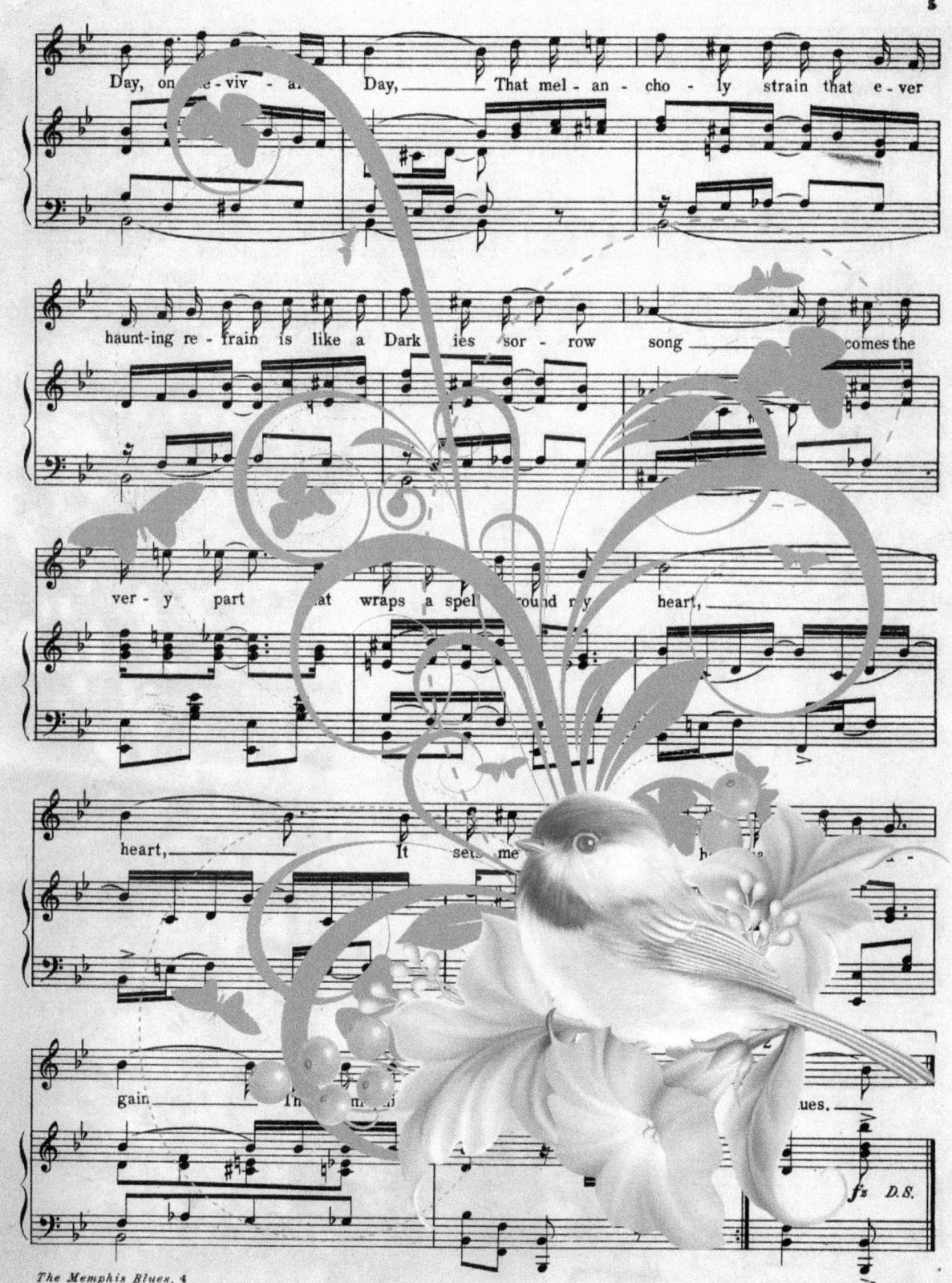

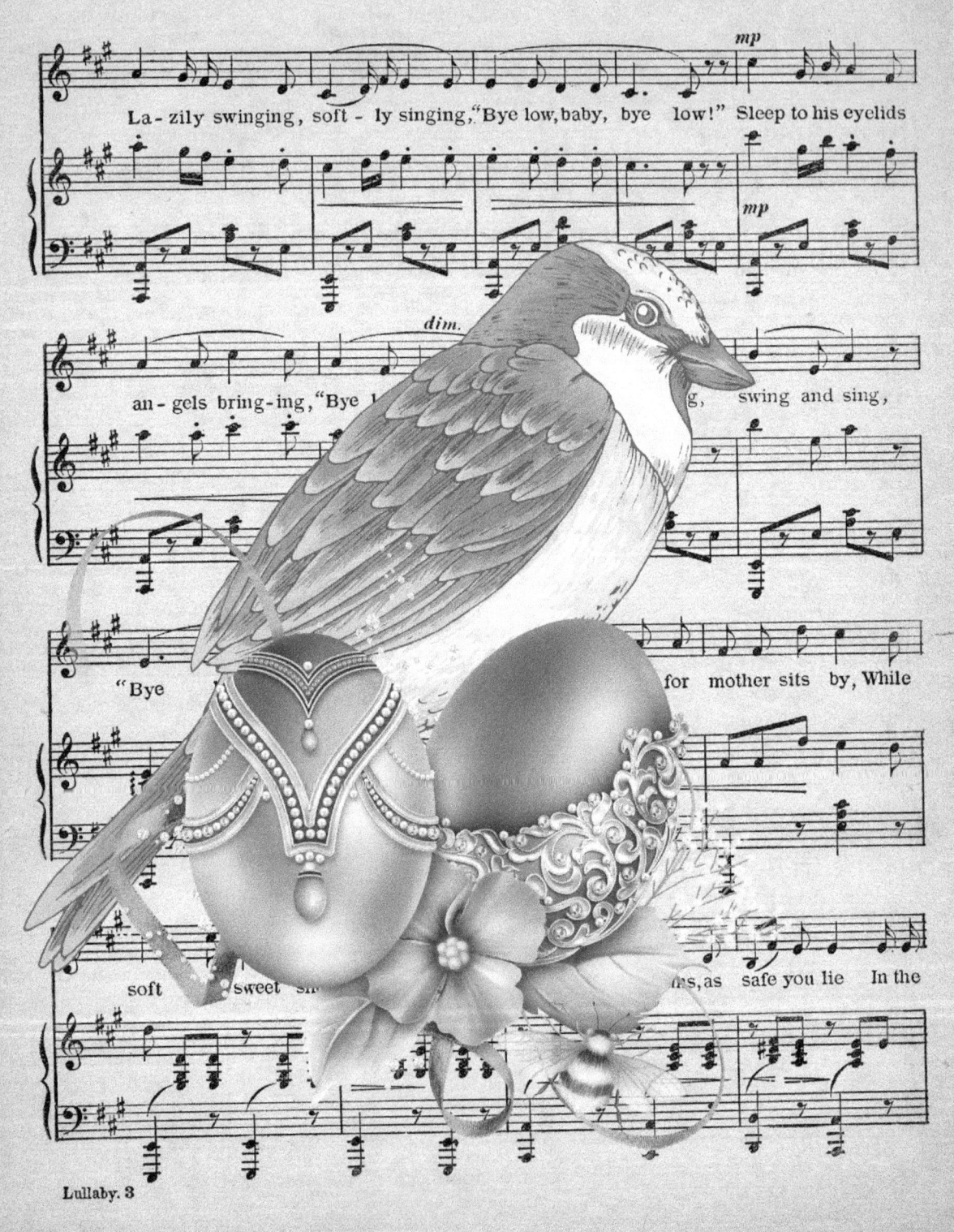

La - zily swinging, soft - ly singing,"Bye low, baby, bye low!" Sleep to his eyelids

an - gels bring-ing,"Bye ... swing and sing,

"Bye ... for mother sits by, While

soft ... sweet ... as, as safe you lie   In the

Lullaby. 3

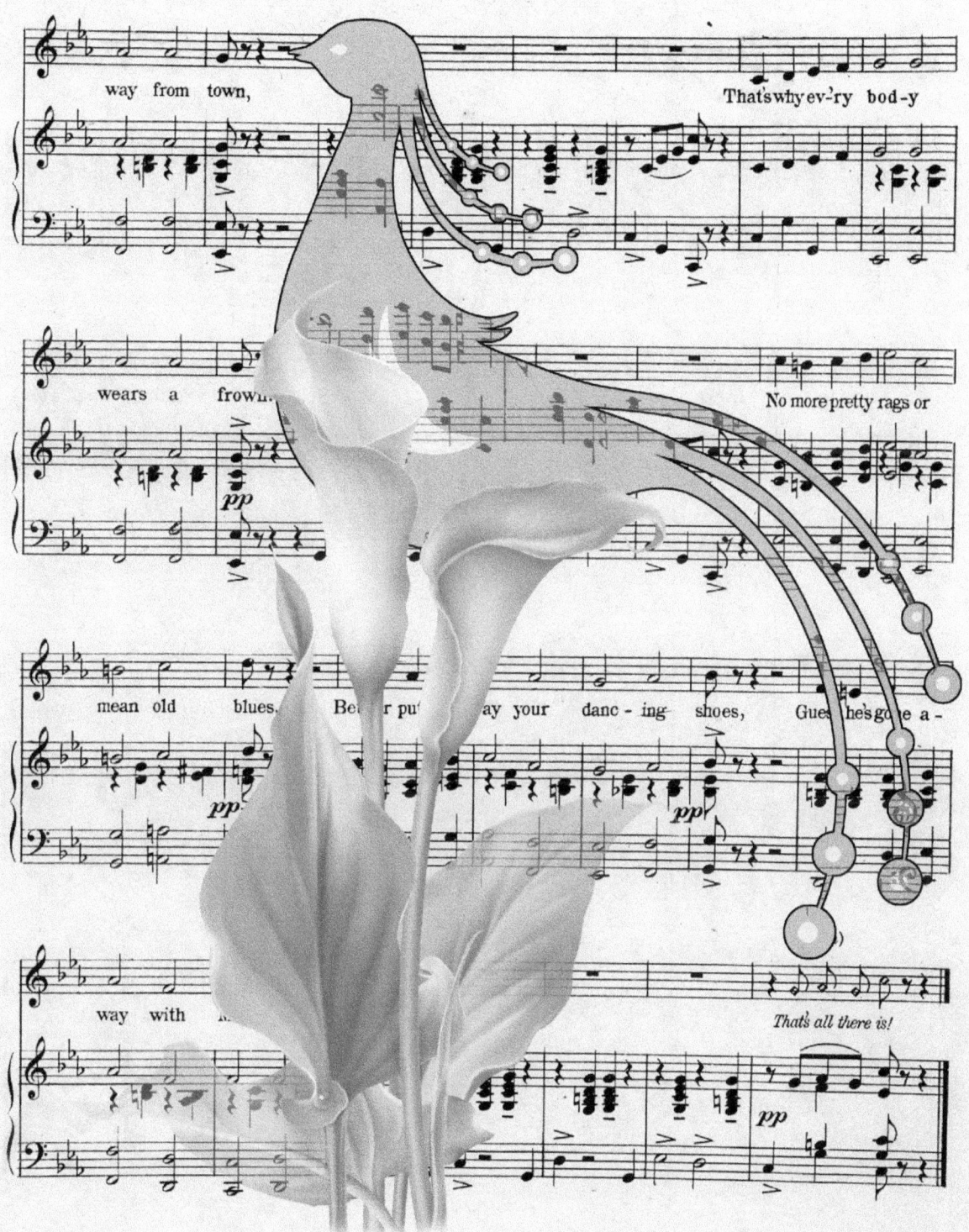

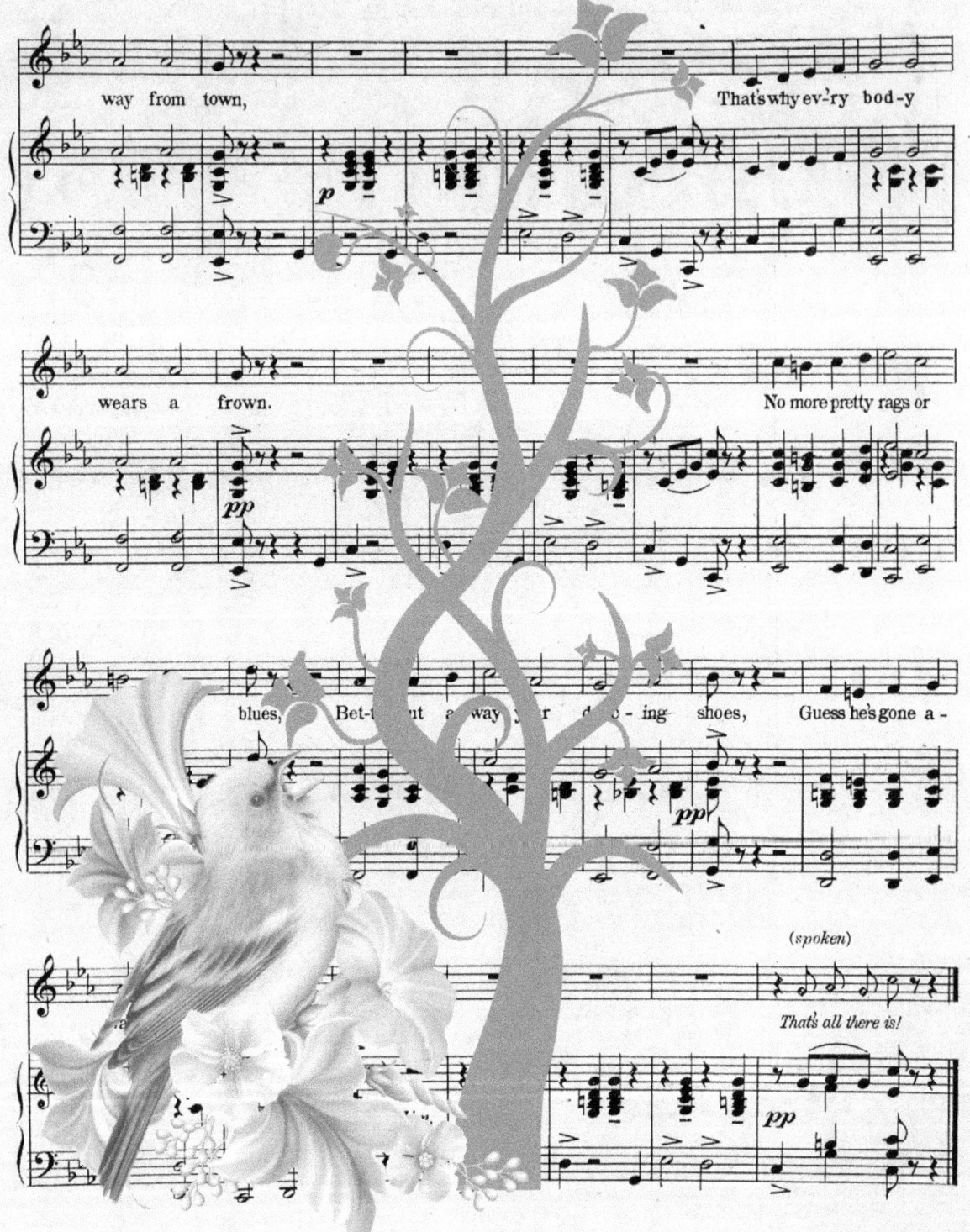

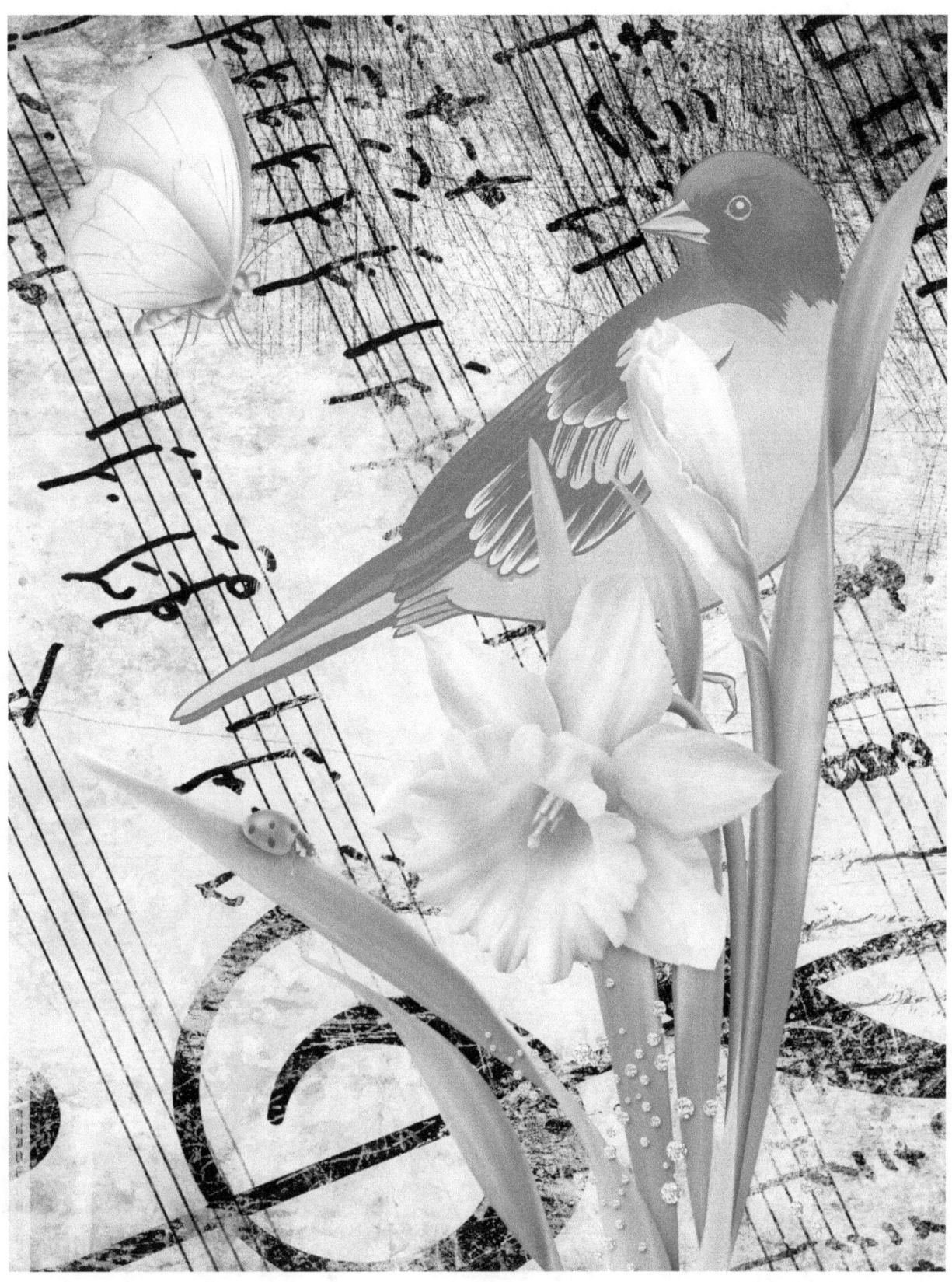

314

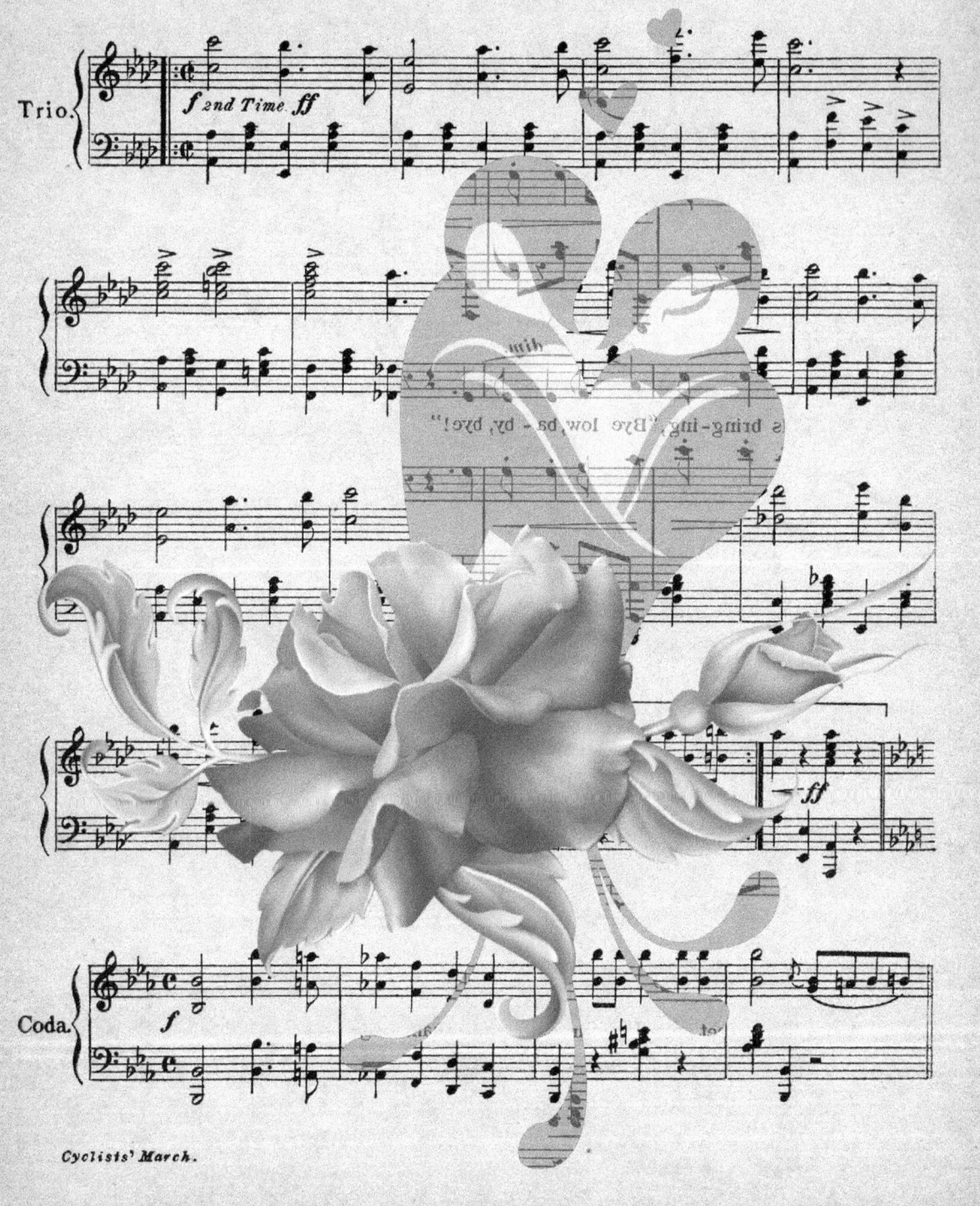

Trio.

f 2nd Time ff

Coda.

f

Cyclists' March.

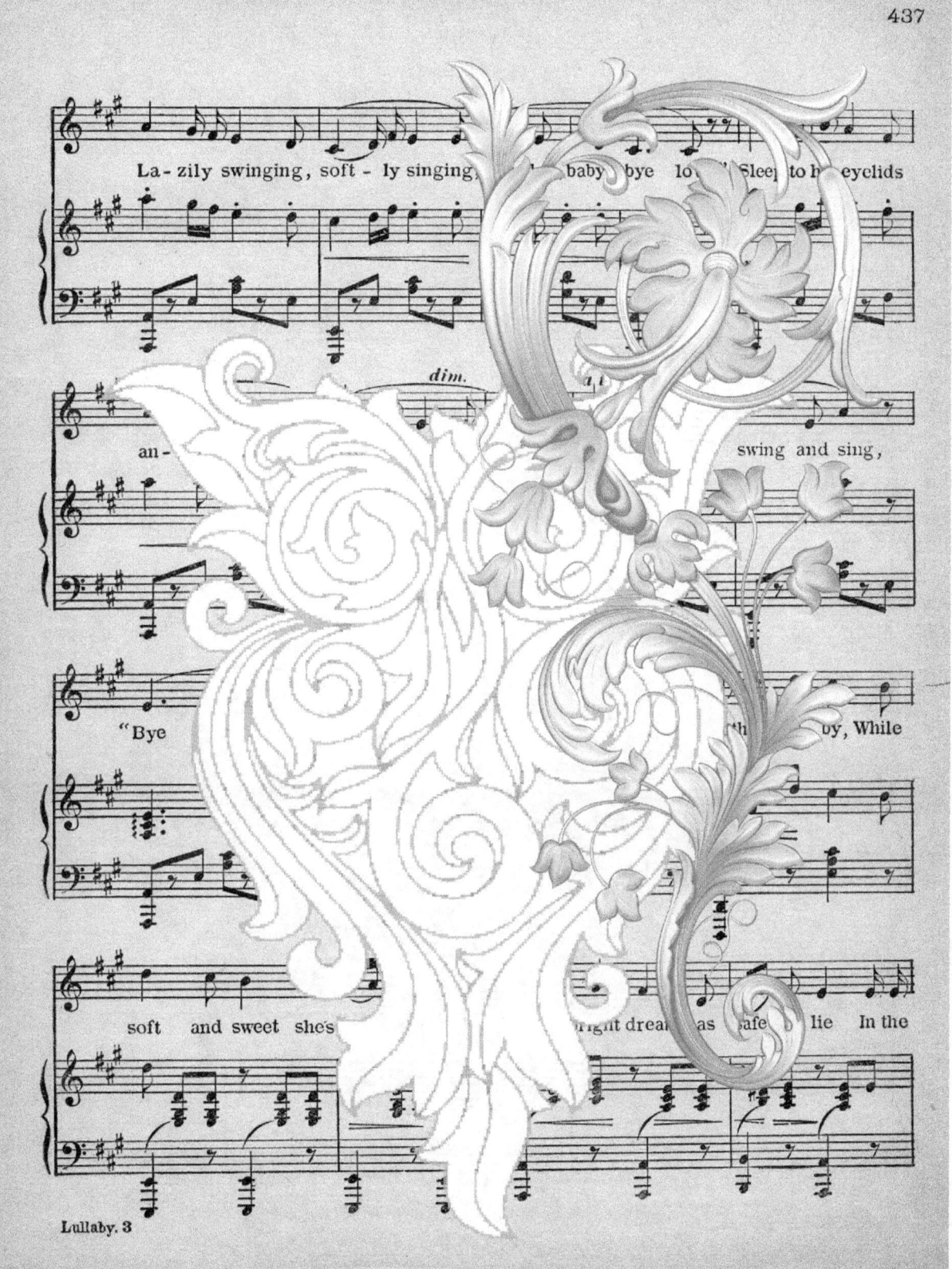

La - zily swinging, soft - ly singing, baby bye lo Sleep to eyelids

an - swing and sing,

"Bye oy, While

soft and sweet she's right drea as safe lie In the

dim.

Lullaby. 3

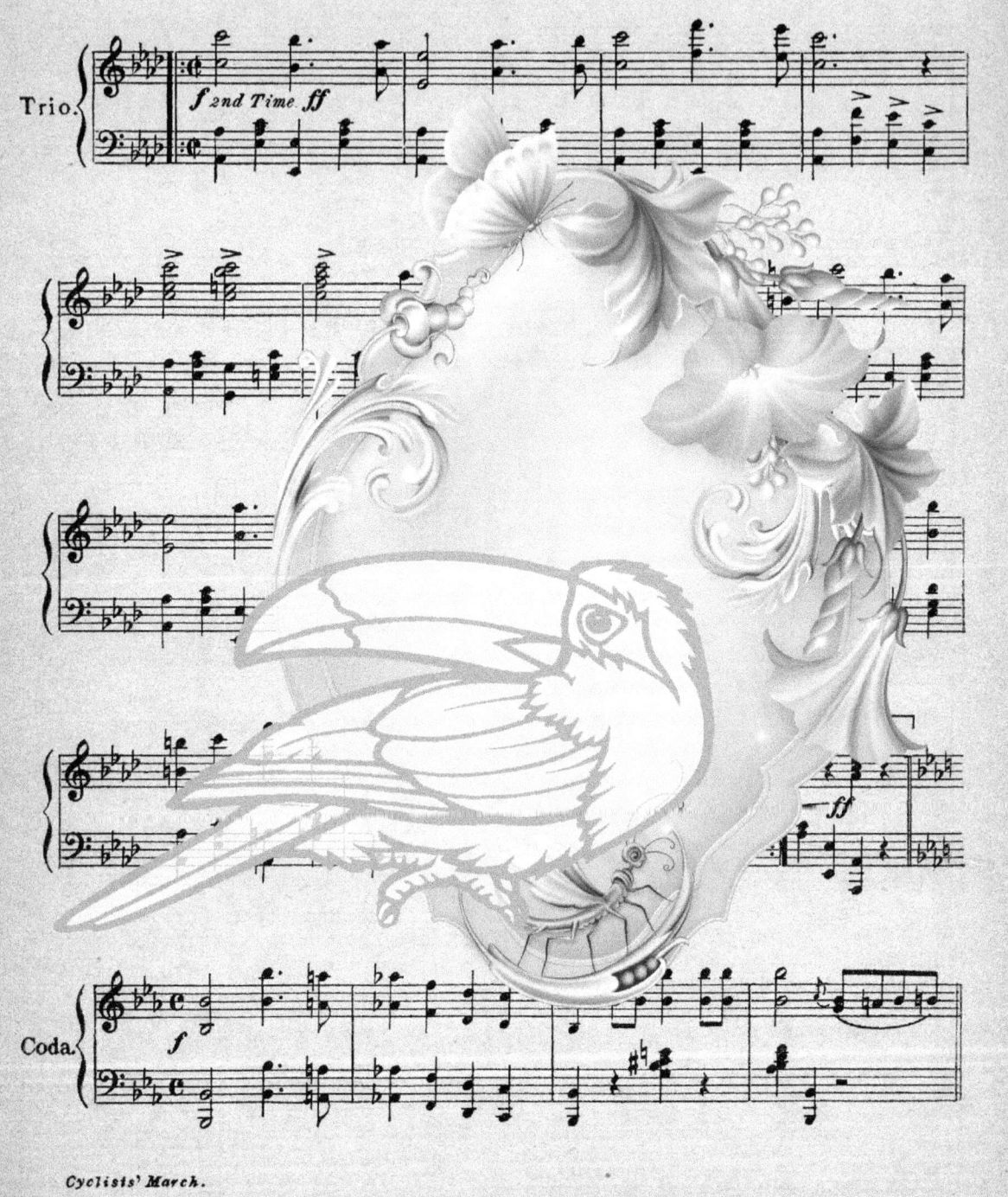

Trio.

f 2nd Time ff

Coda.

f

Cyclists' March.

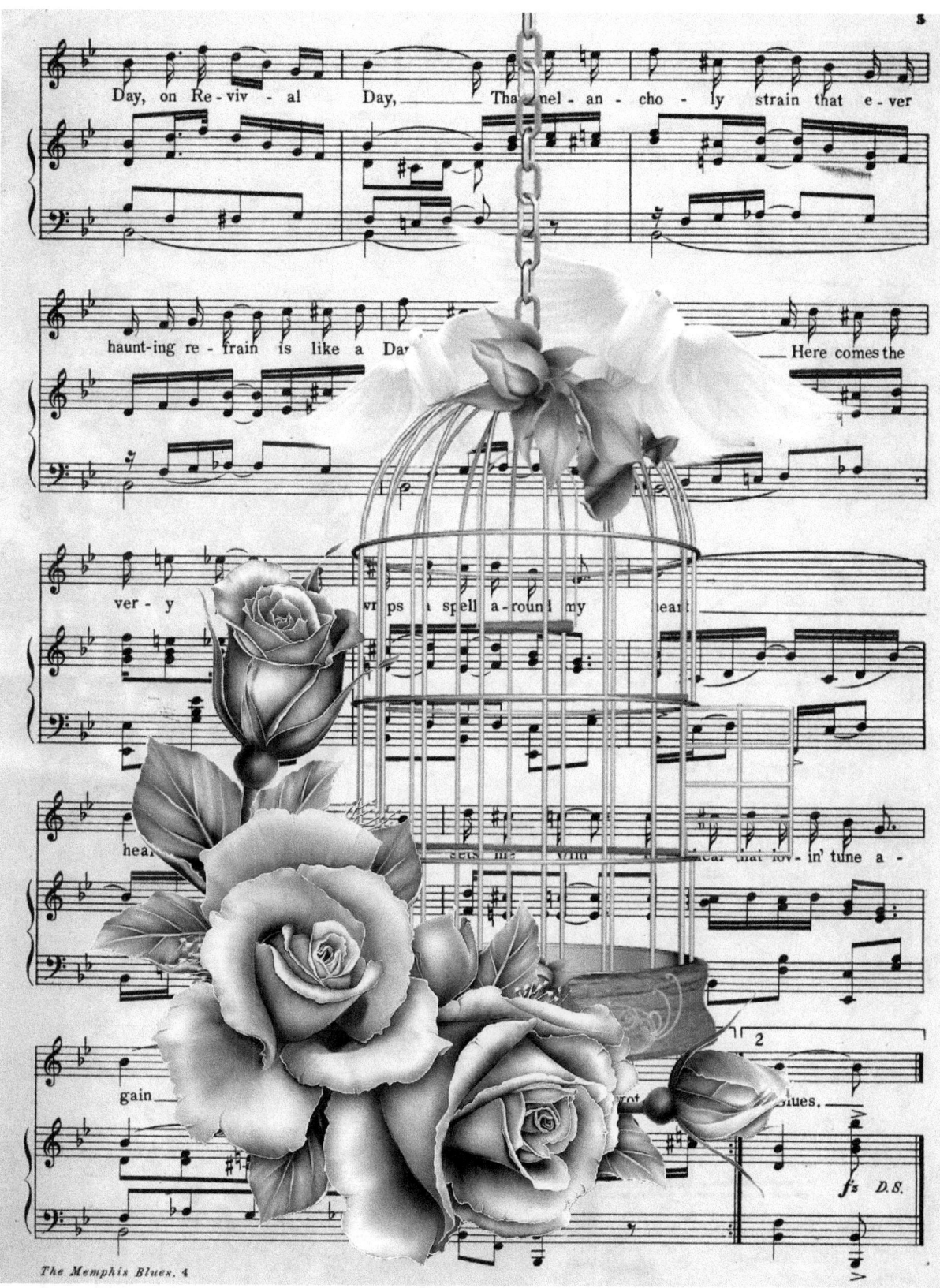

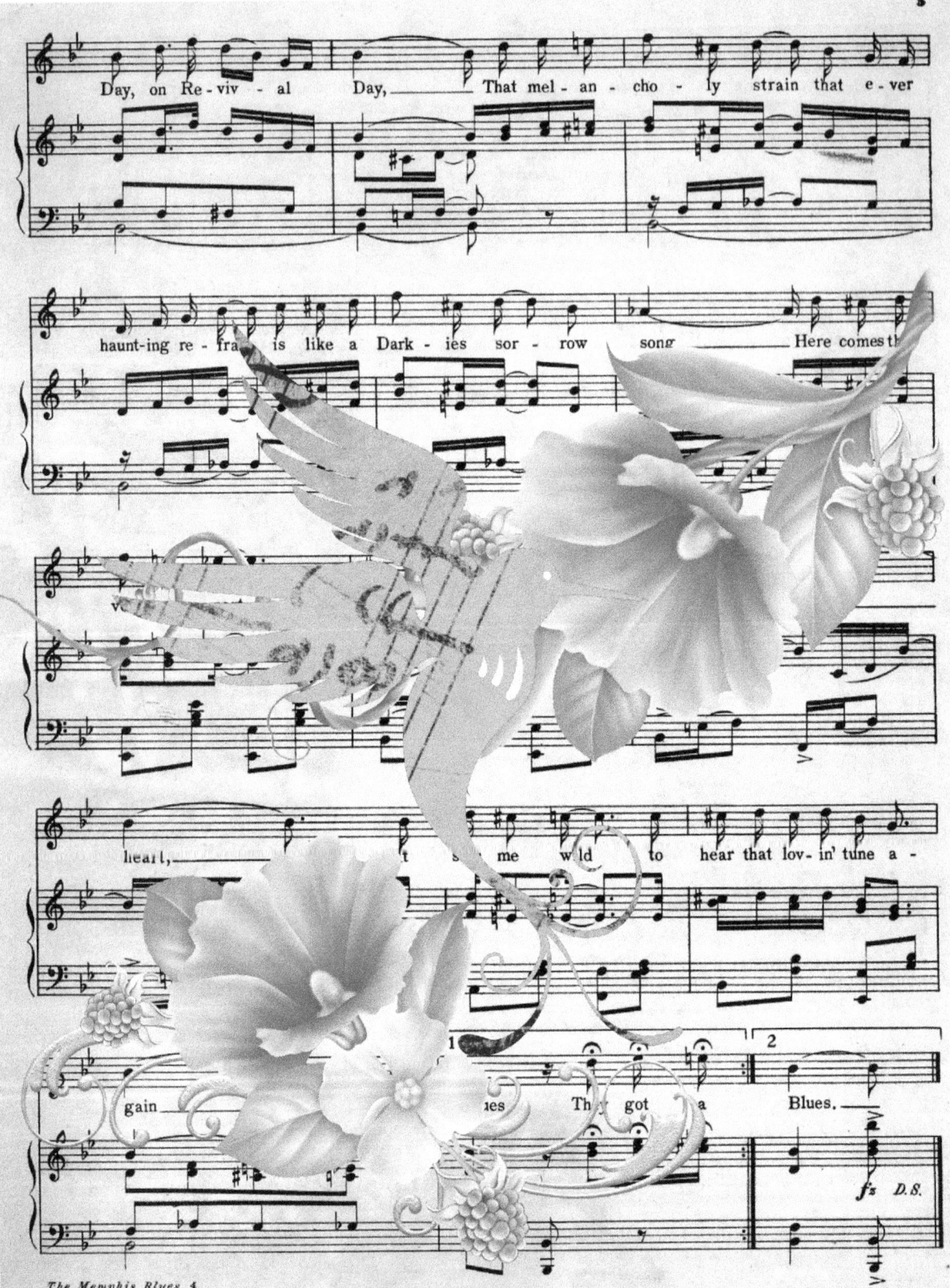

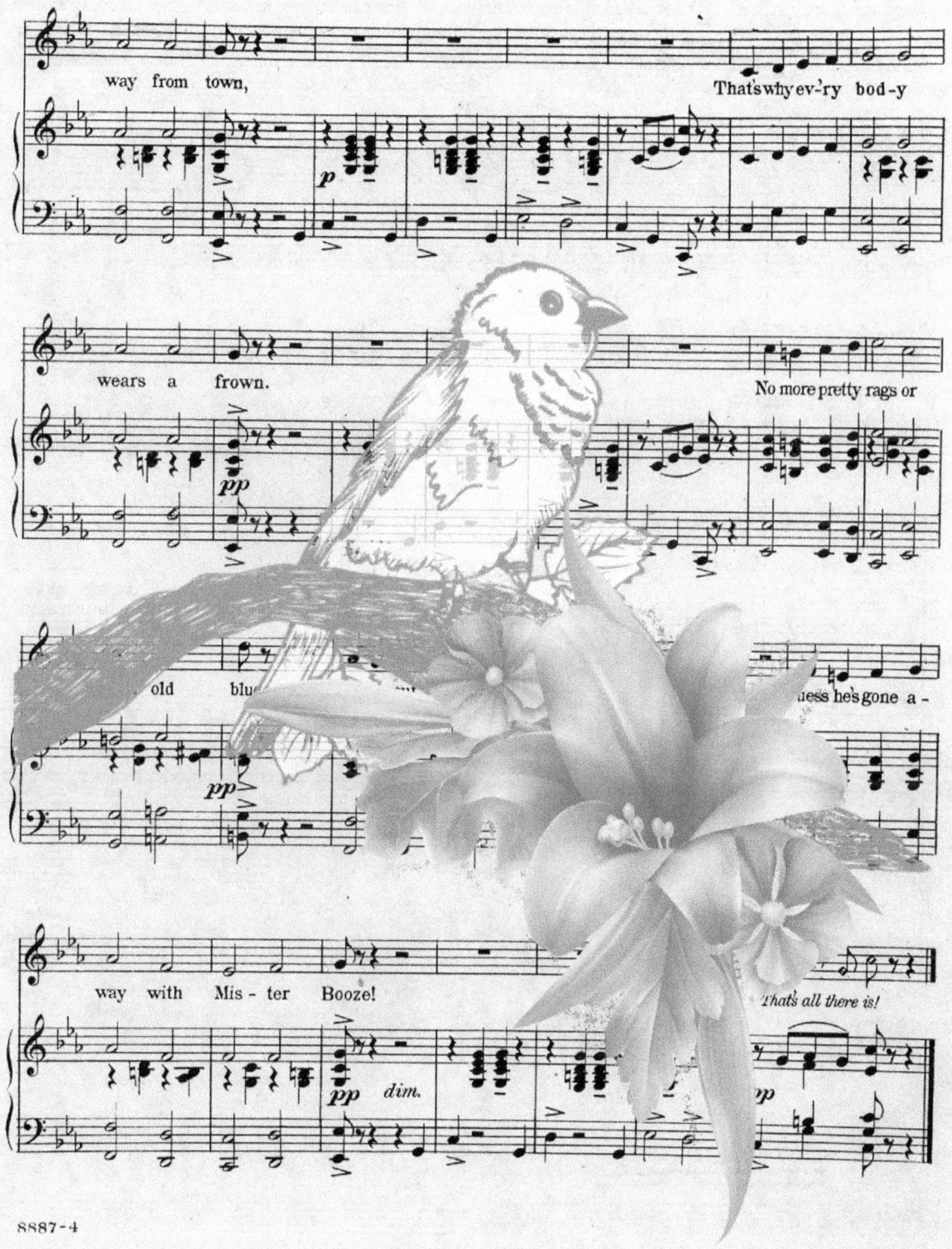

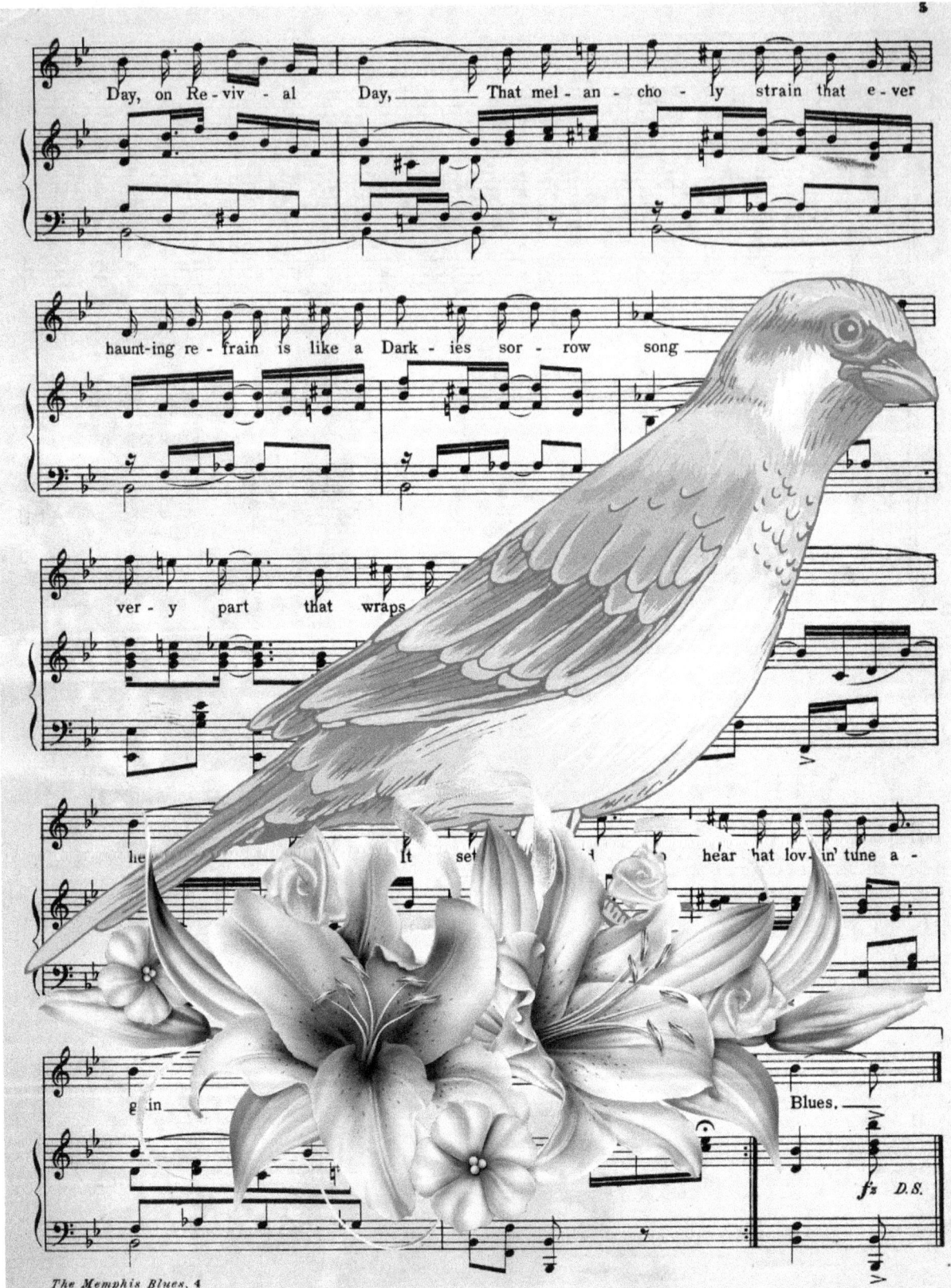

Day, on Re - viv - al   Day, _____   That mel - an - cho - ly   strain that e - ver

haunt-ing re - frain is like a Dark - ies sor - row   song _____

ver - y   part   that   wraps

he _____   It   set   hear that lov - in' tune a -

g in   Blues.

fz D.S.

The Memphis Blues. 4

314

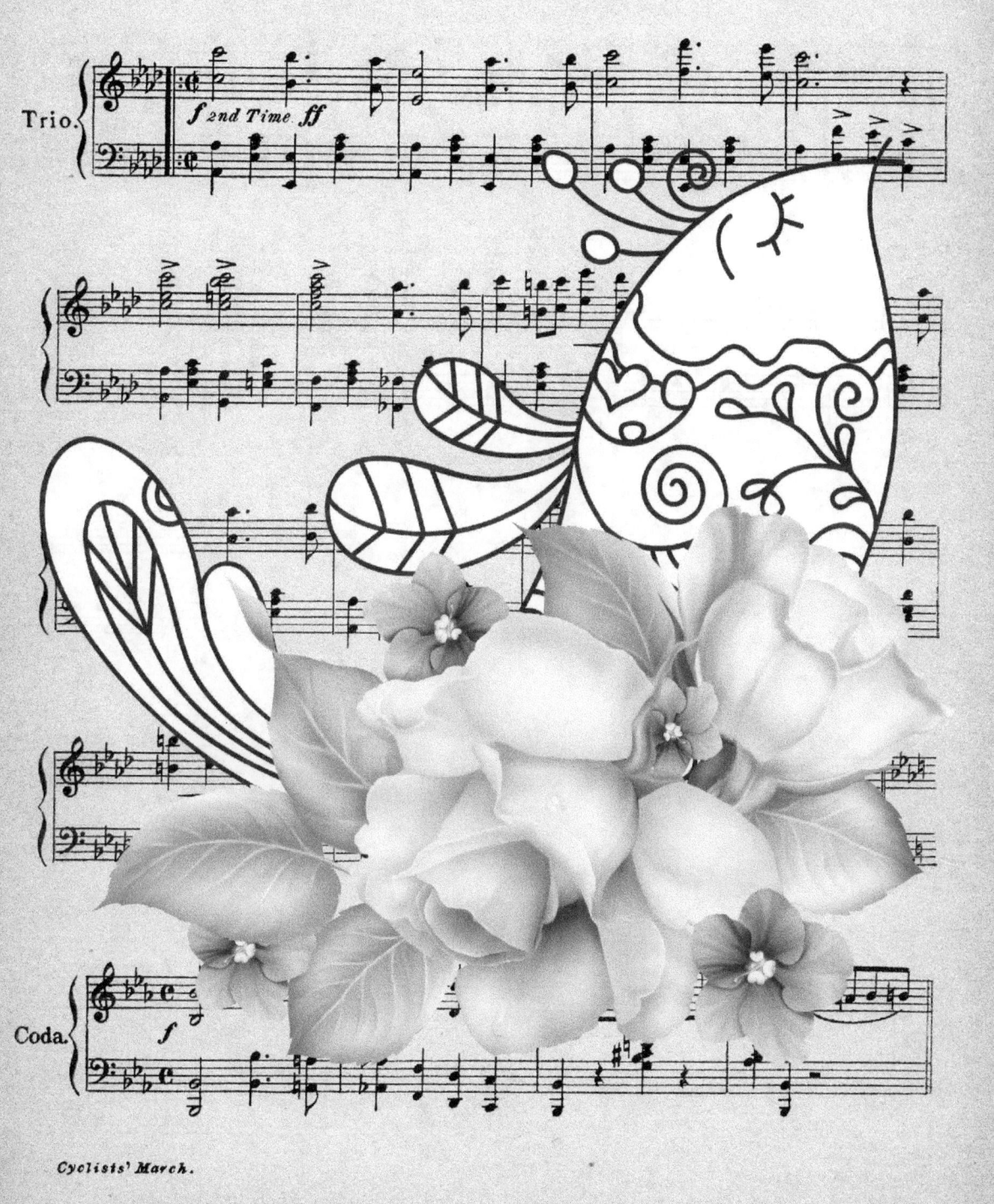

Trio.

f 2nd Time *ff*

Coda. *f*

Cyclists' March.

314

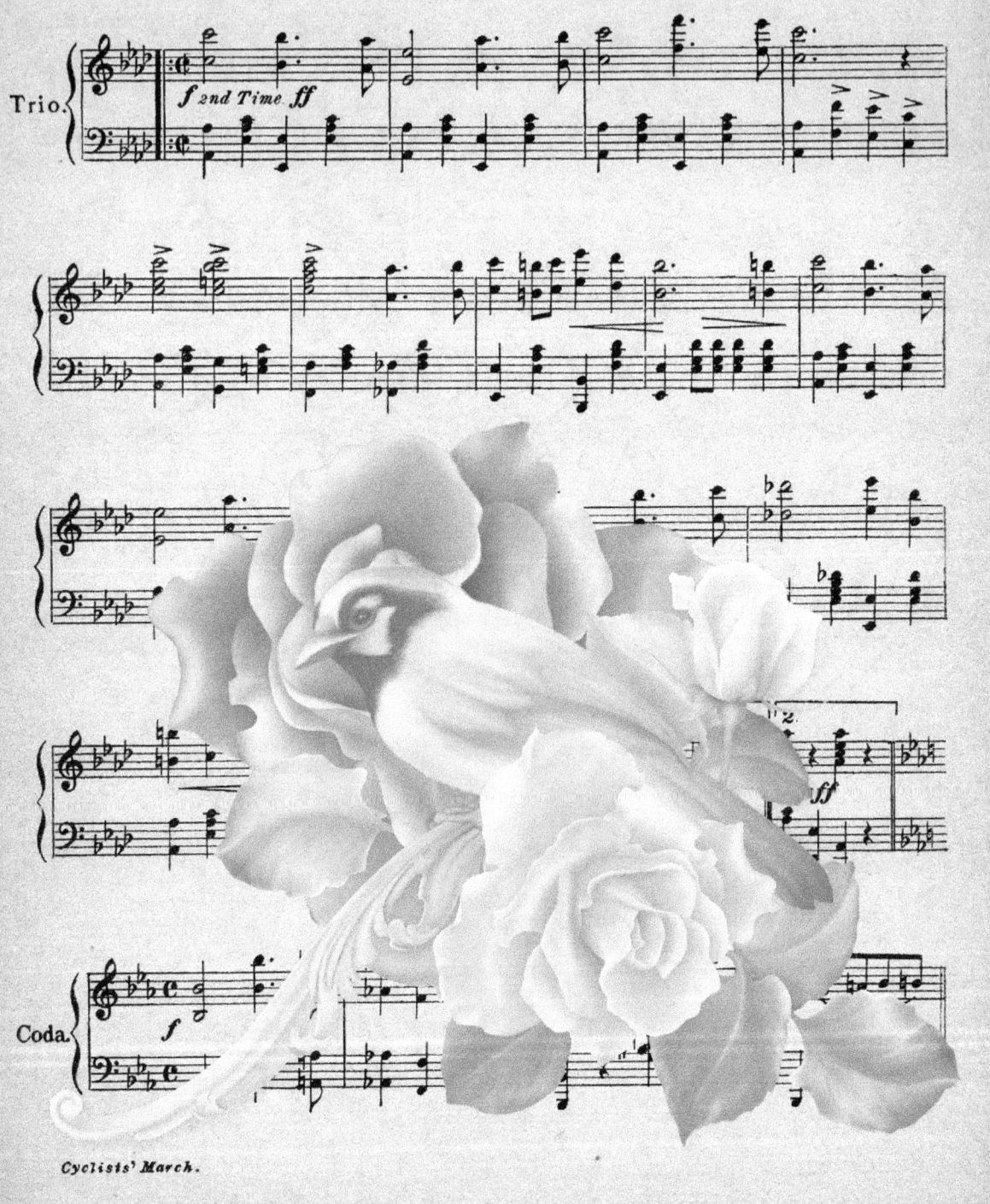

Trio.

Coda.

Cyclists' March.

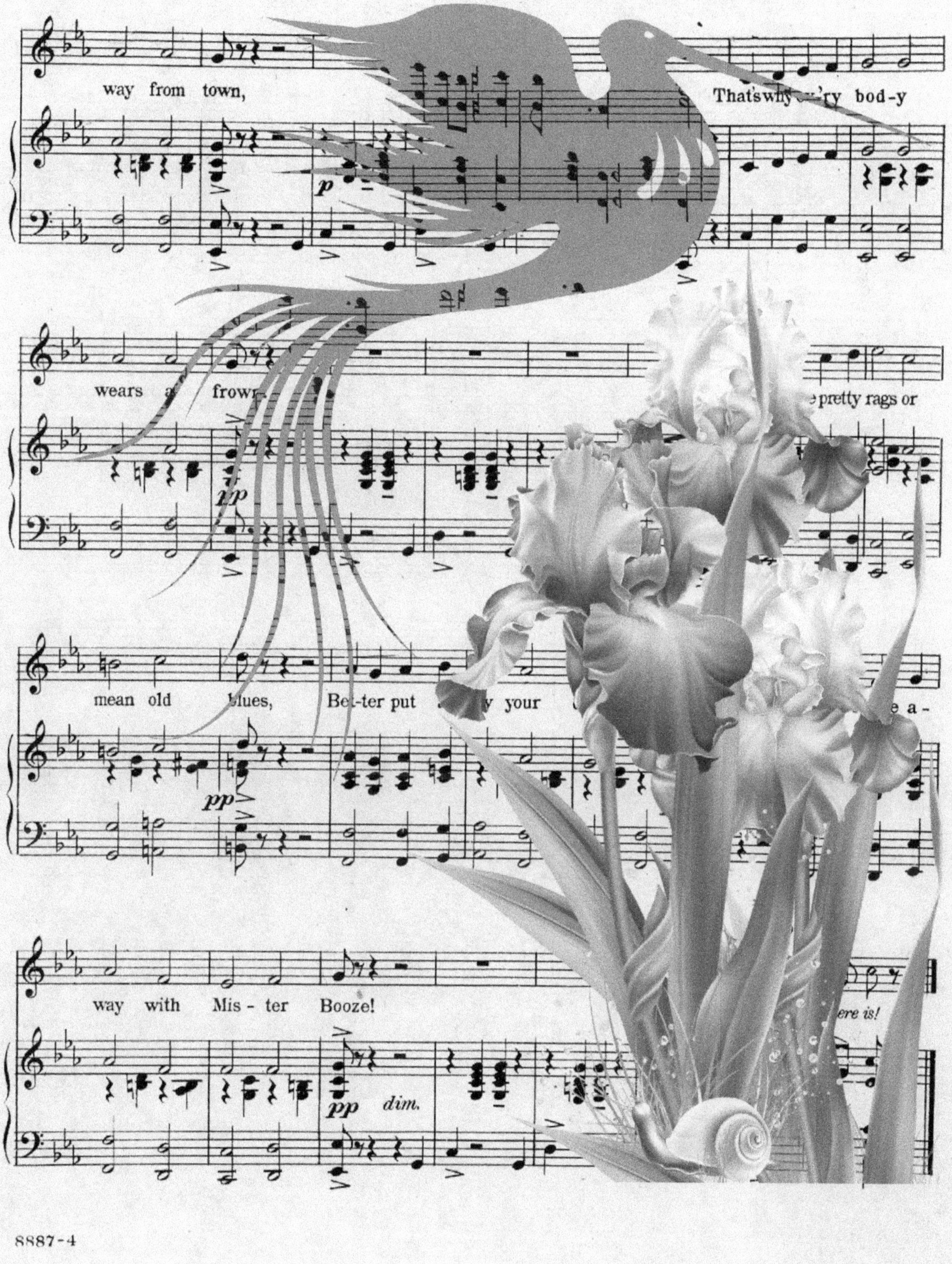

way from town,   That's why ev'ry bod-y

wears a frown,   the pretty rags or

mean old blues,   Bet-ter put away your   e a-

way with Mis-ter Booze!   ere is!

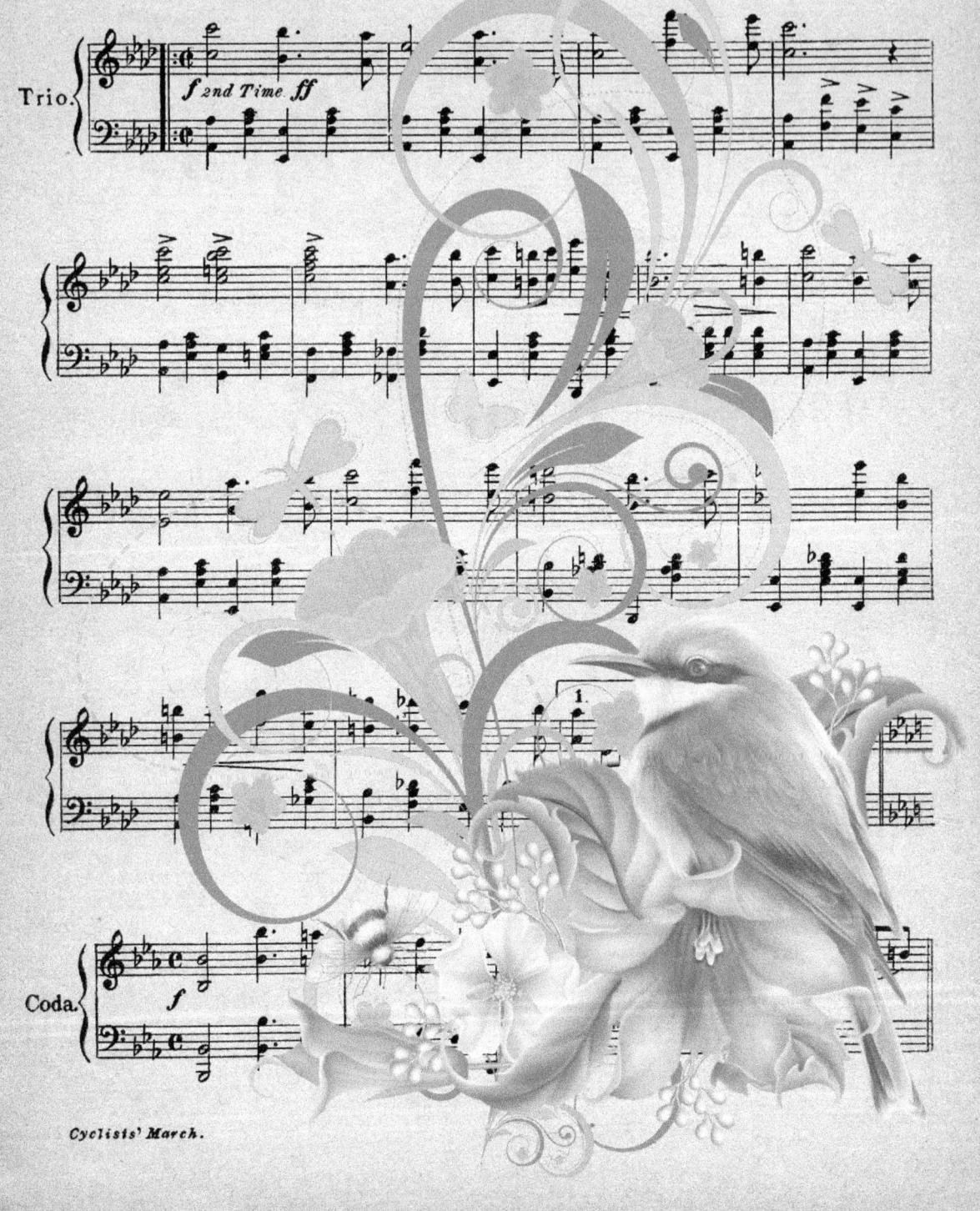

Trio.

f 2nd Time ff

Coda.

f

Cyclists' March.

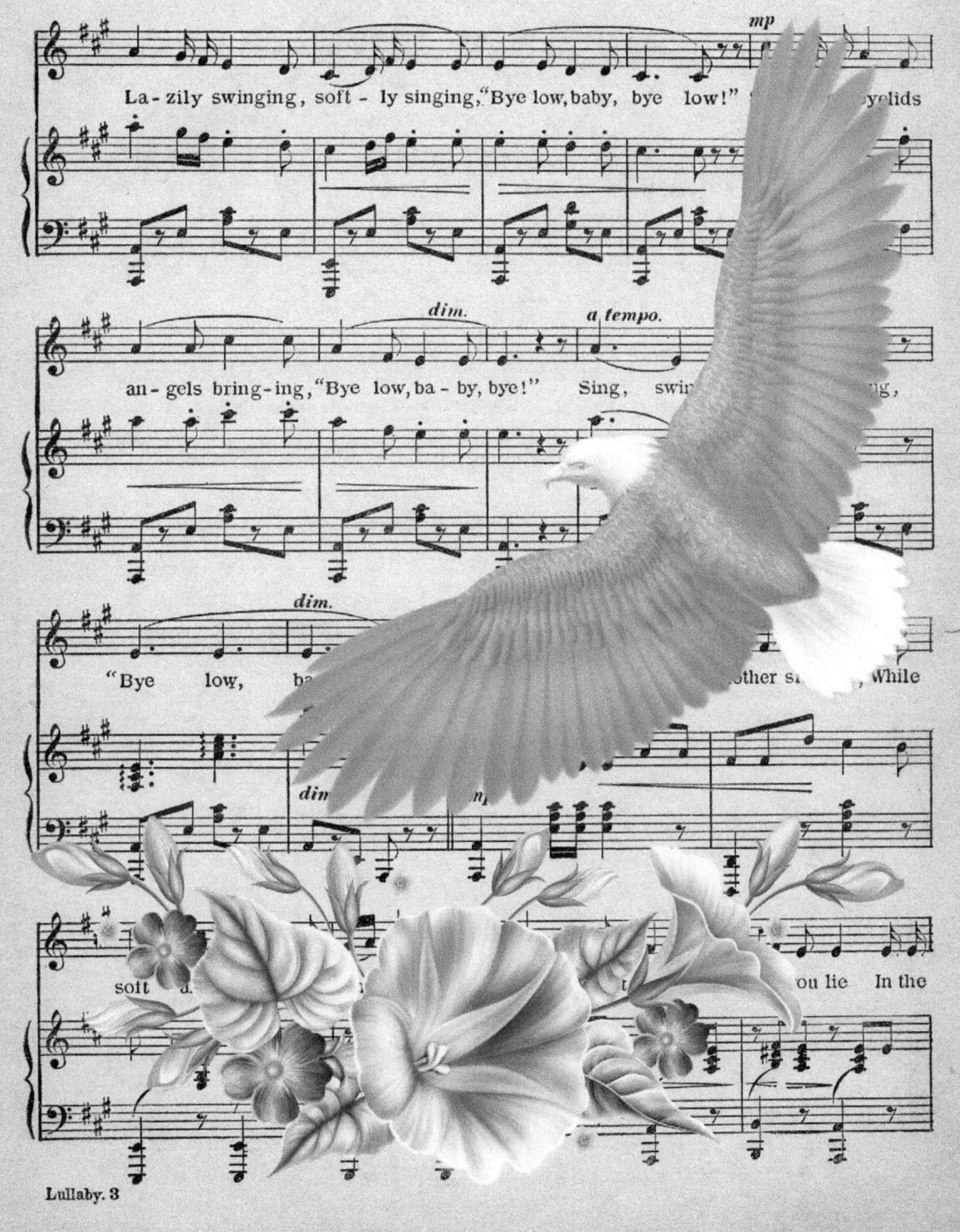

La - zily swinging, soft - ly singing, "Bye low, baby, bye low!" ... eyelids

an - gels bring-ing, "Bye low, ba - by, bye!" Sing, swin... ...ng,

"Bye low, ba... ...other s... , while

soft... ...ou lie In the

Lullaby. 3

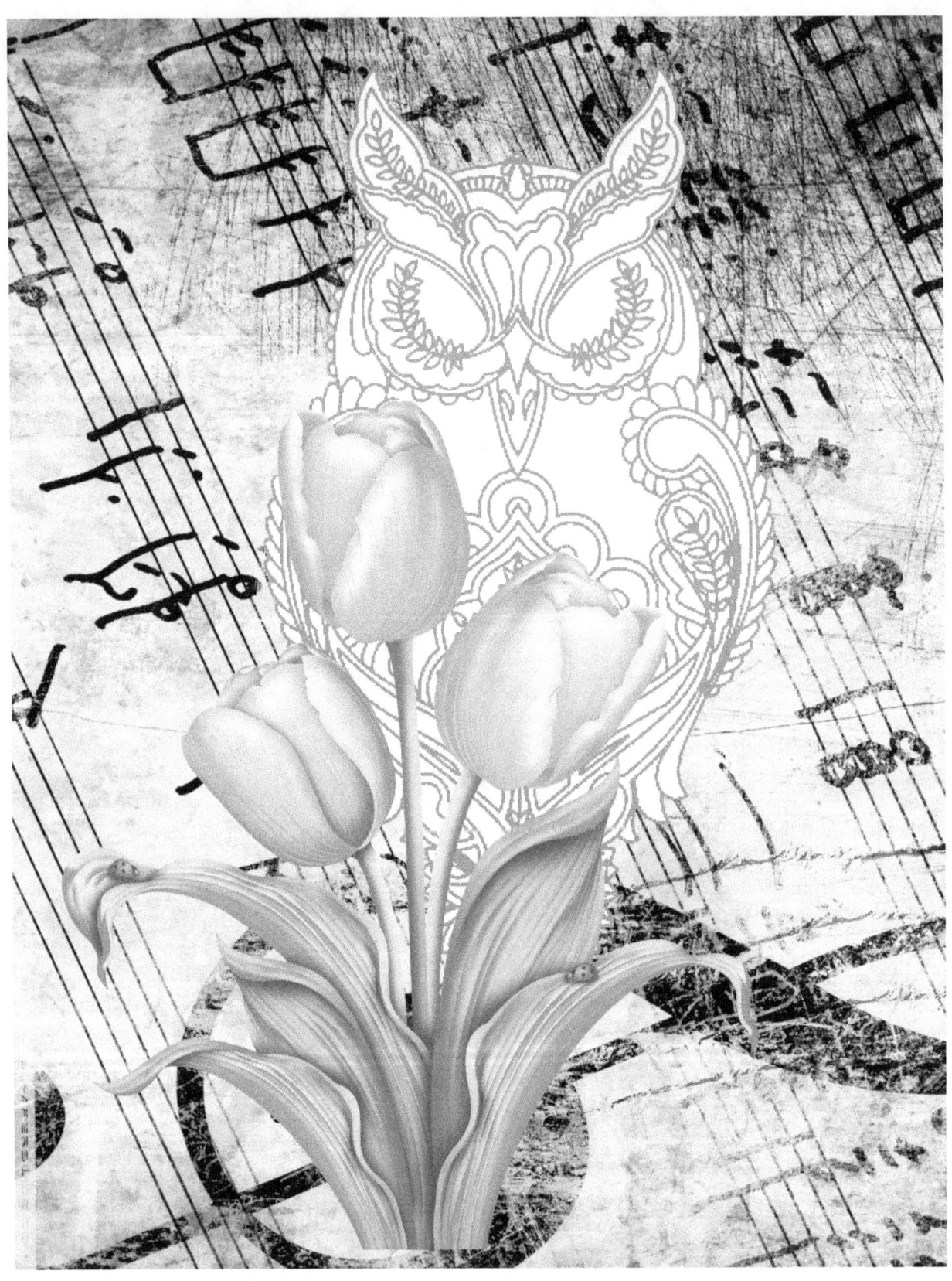

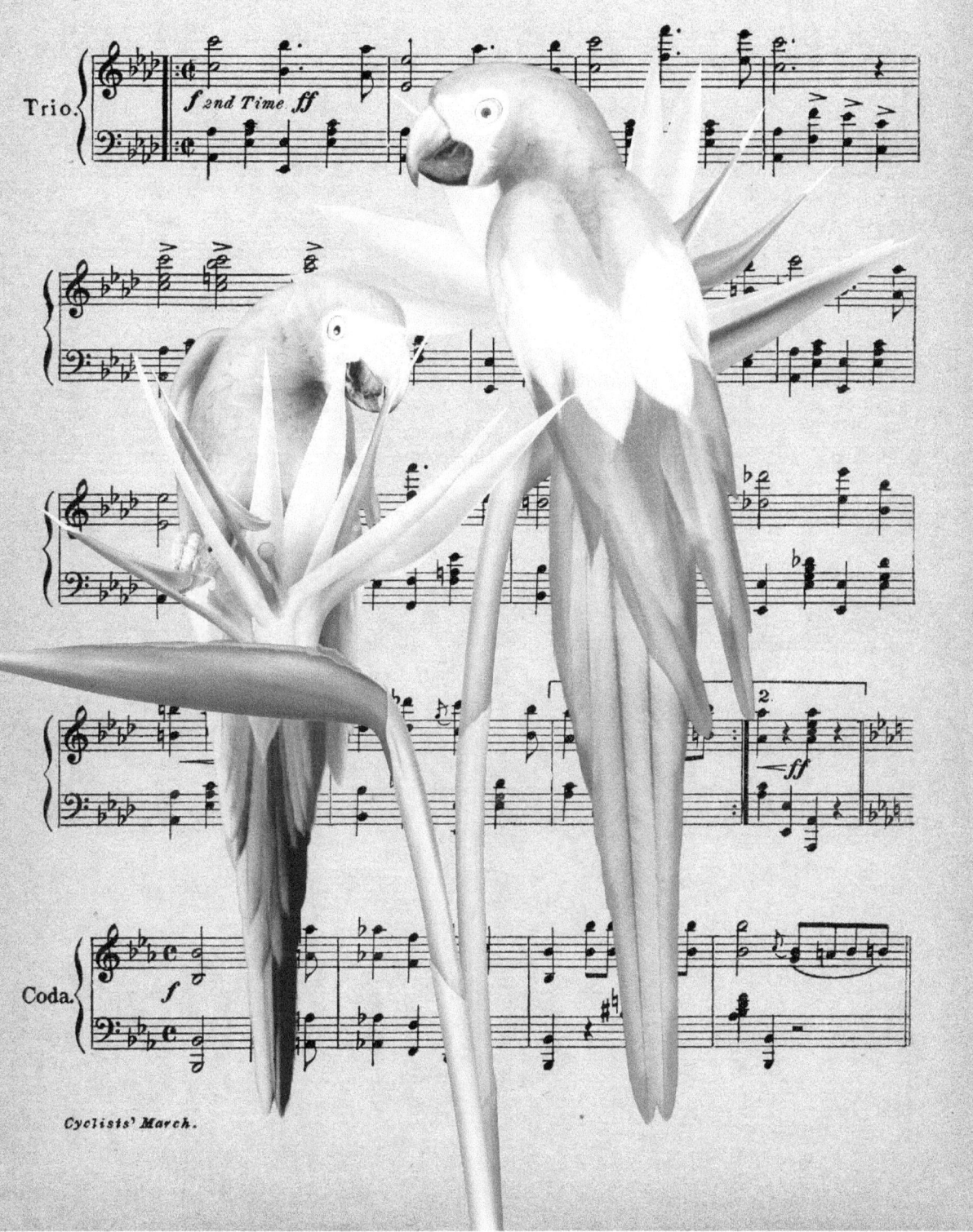

Trio.

Coda.

Cyclists' March.

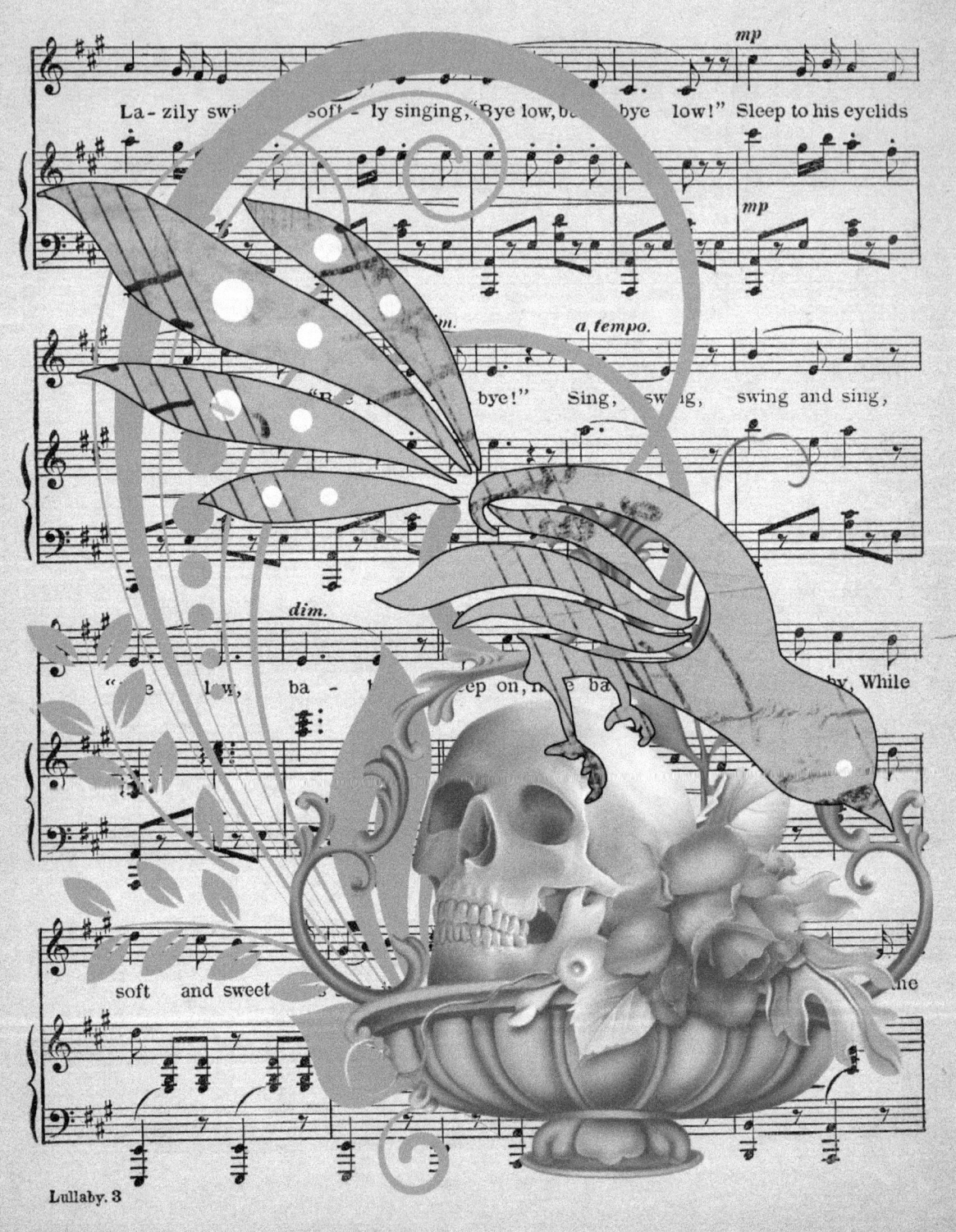

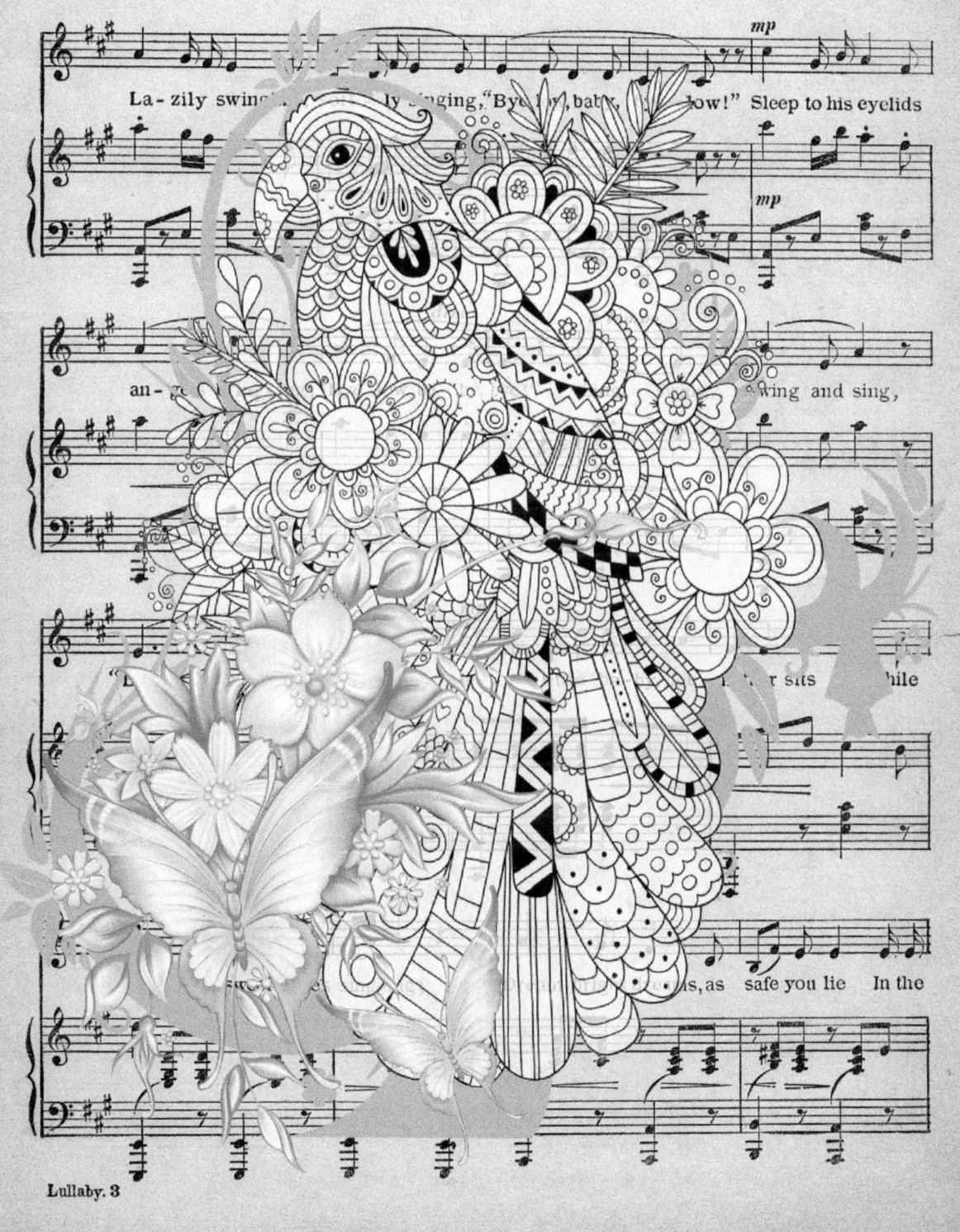

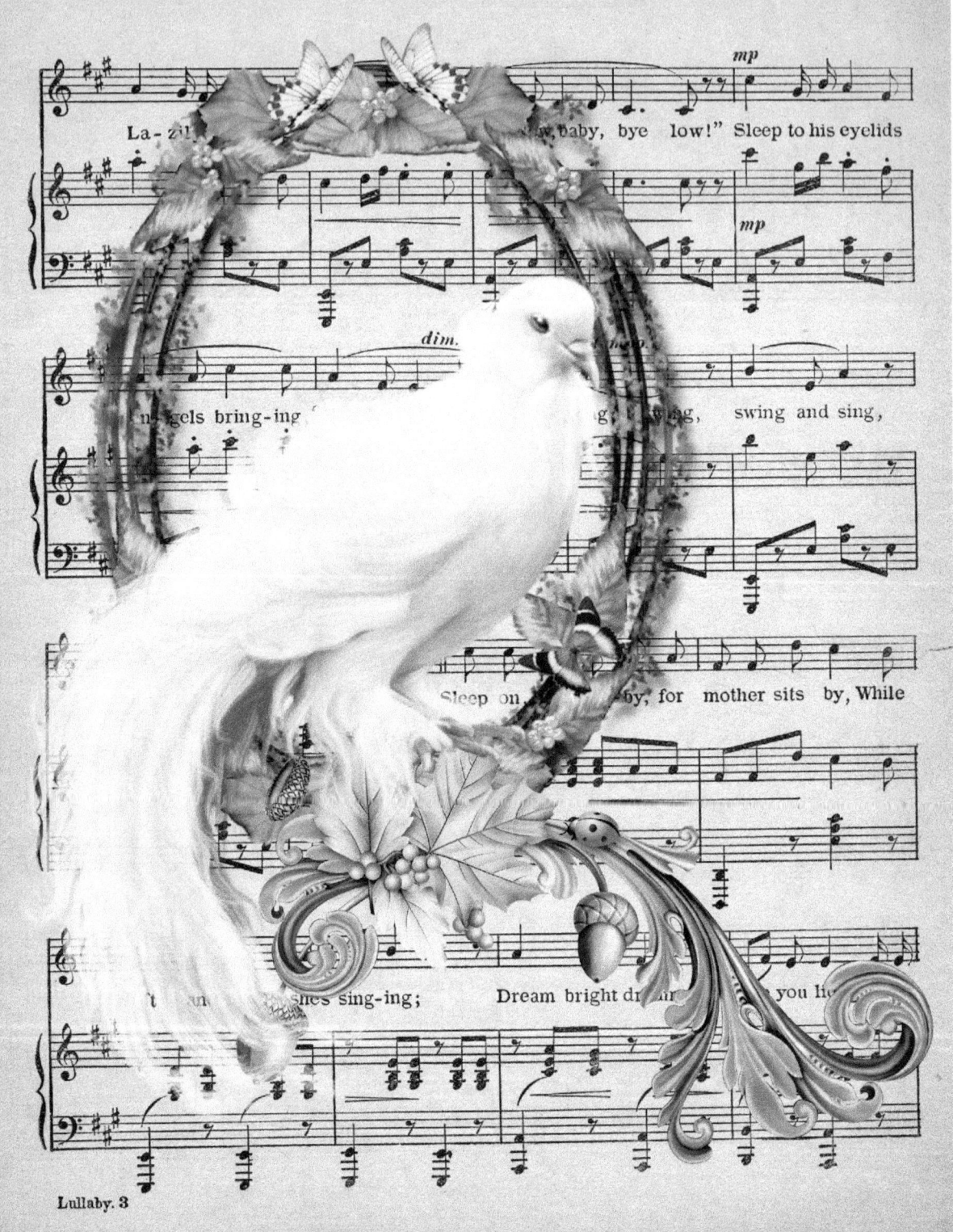

Lullaby. 3

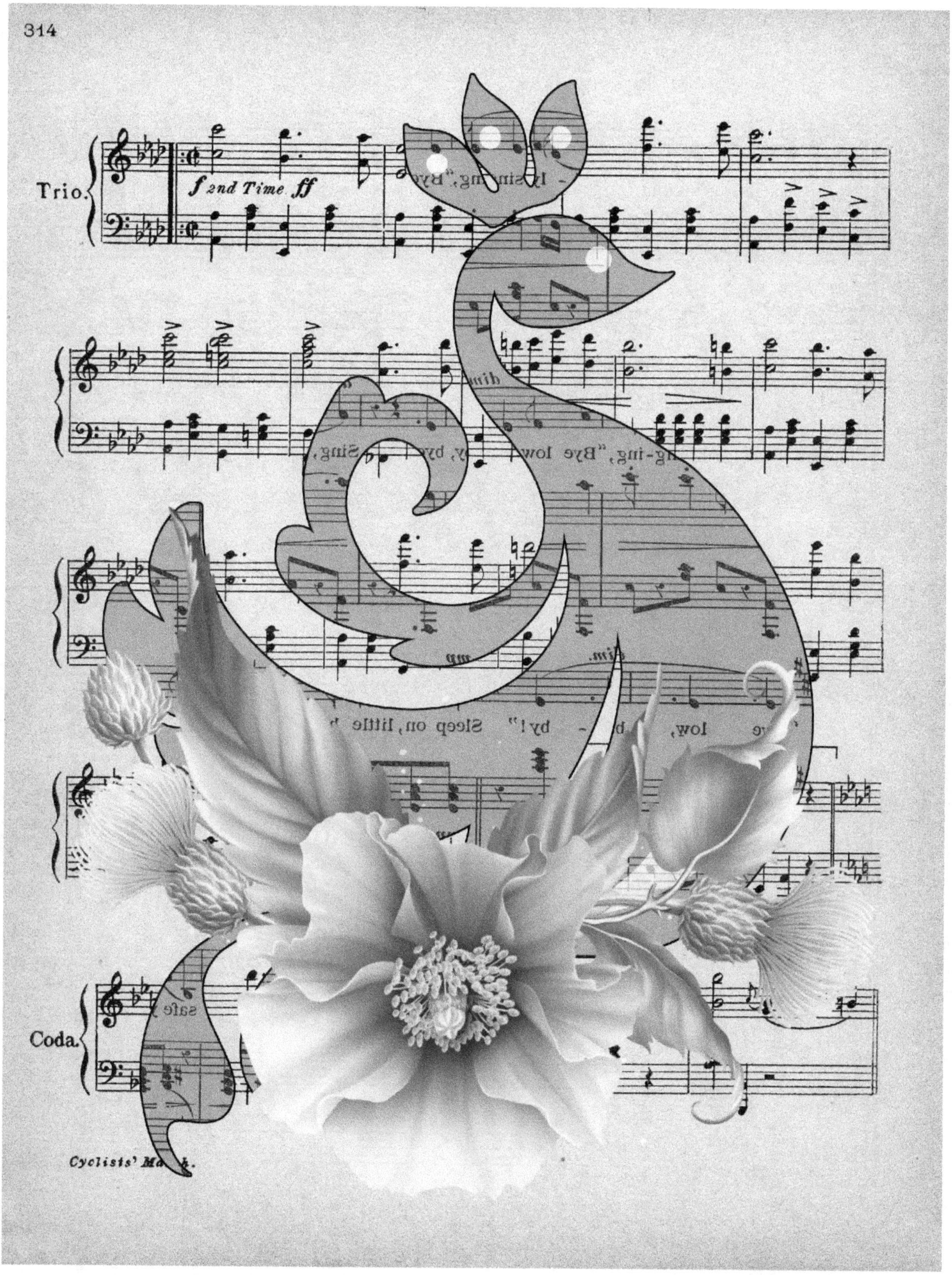
314
Trio.
f 2nd Time ff
Coda.
Cyclists' March.

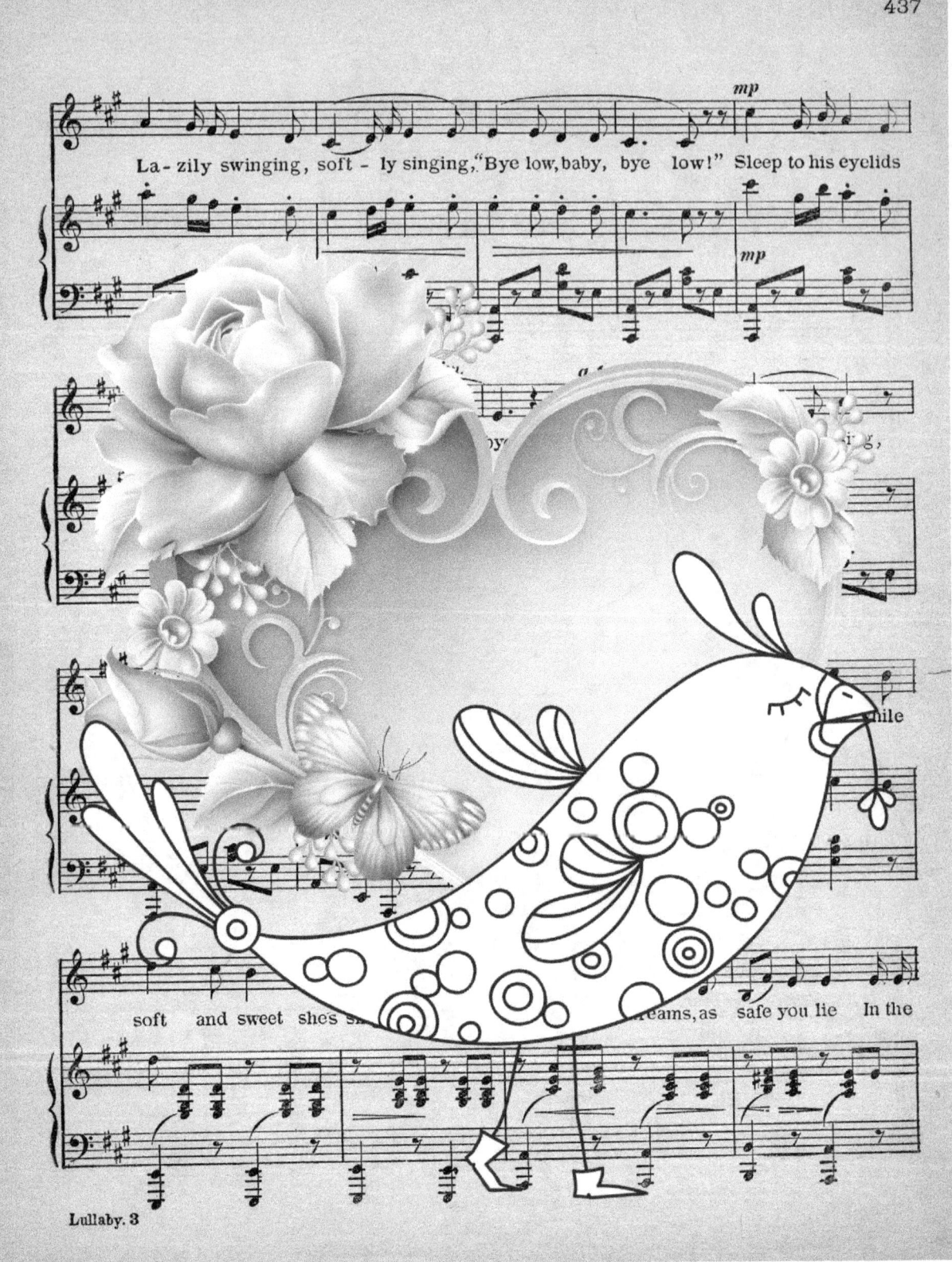

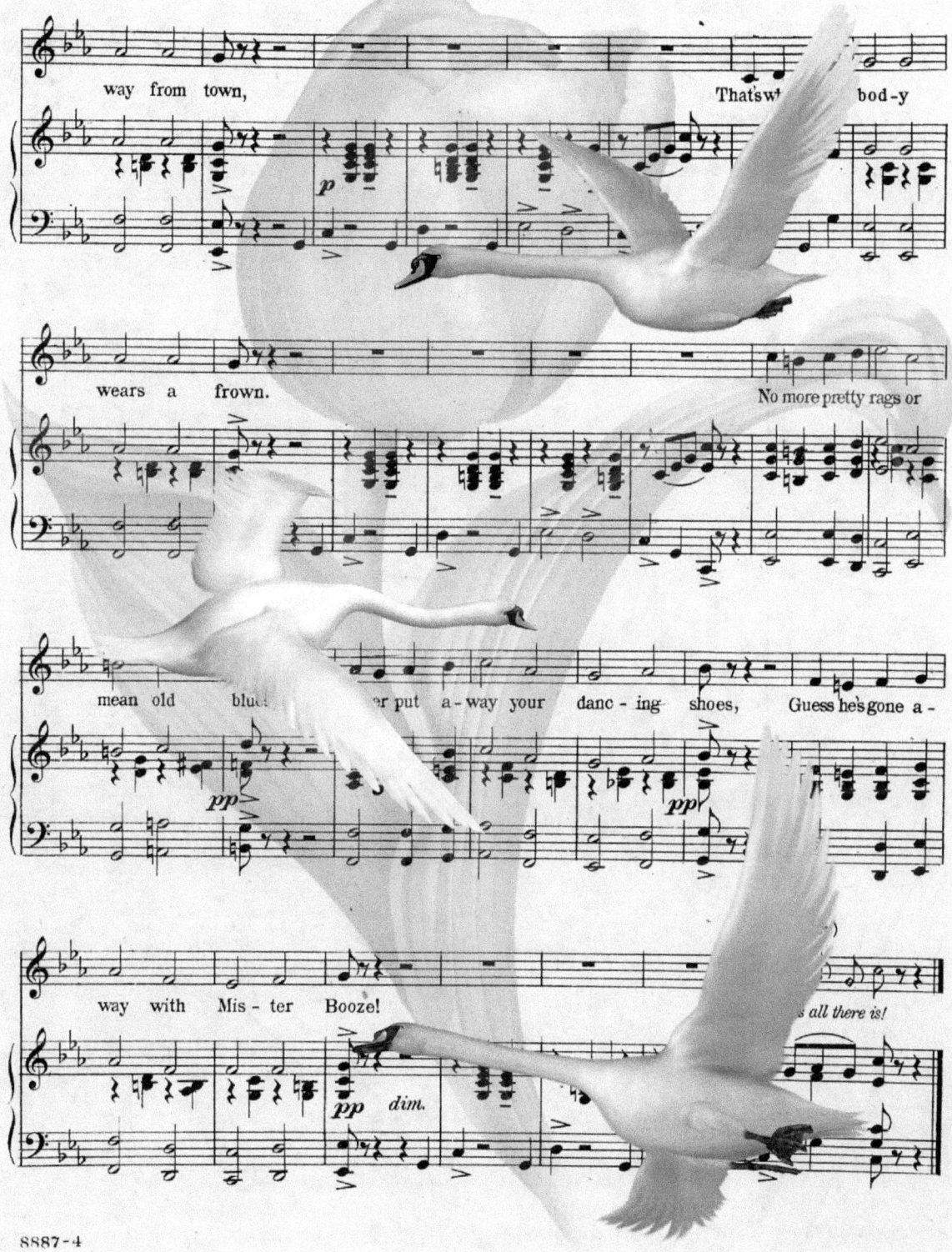

way from town,   That's wh bod-y

wears a frown.   No more pretty rags or

mean old blue   er put a-way your danc-ing shoes, Guess he's gone a-

way with Mis-ter Booze!   s all there is!

p

pp

pp

pp dim.

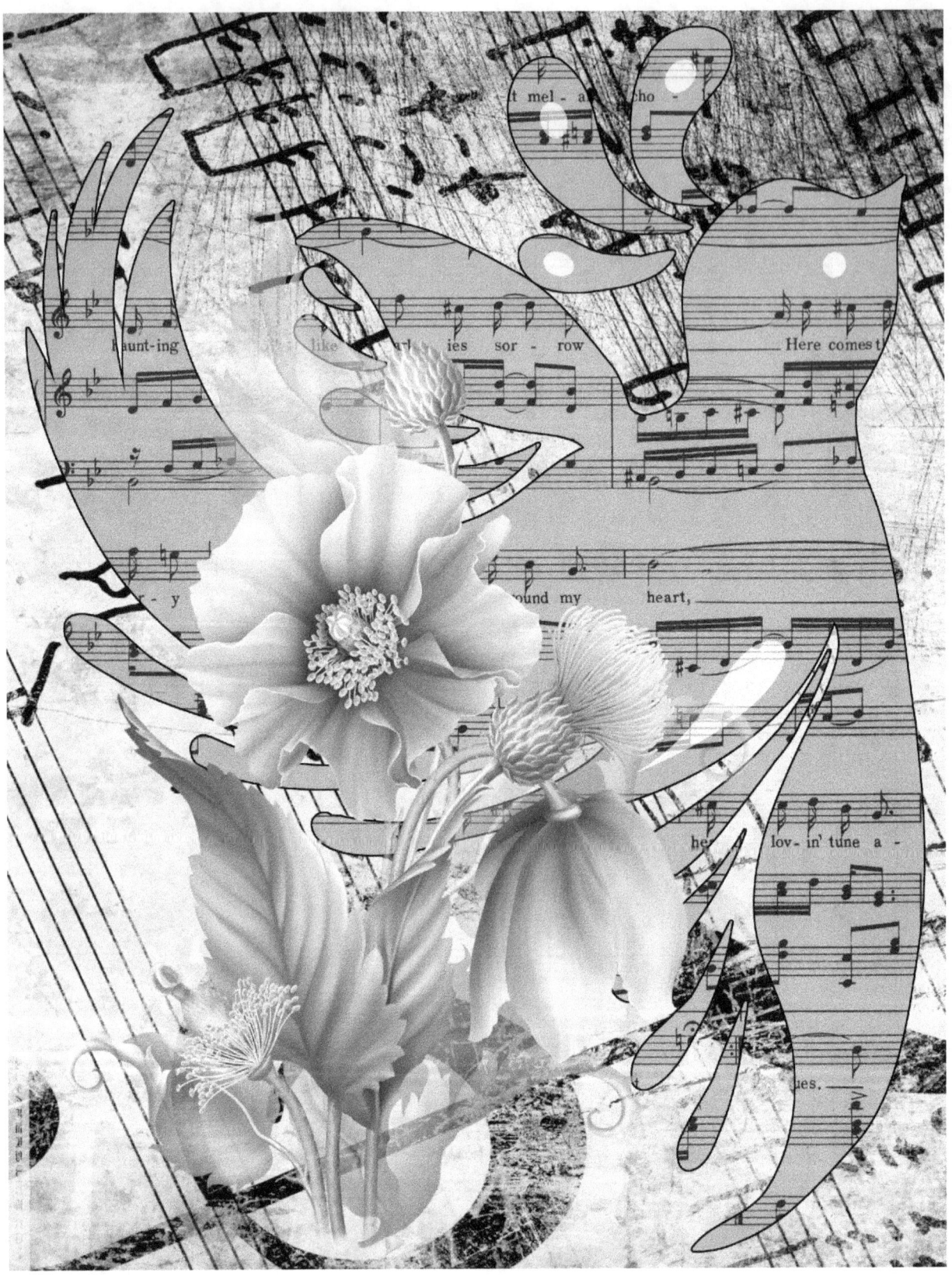

314

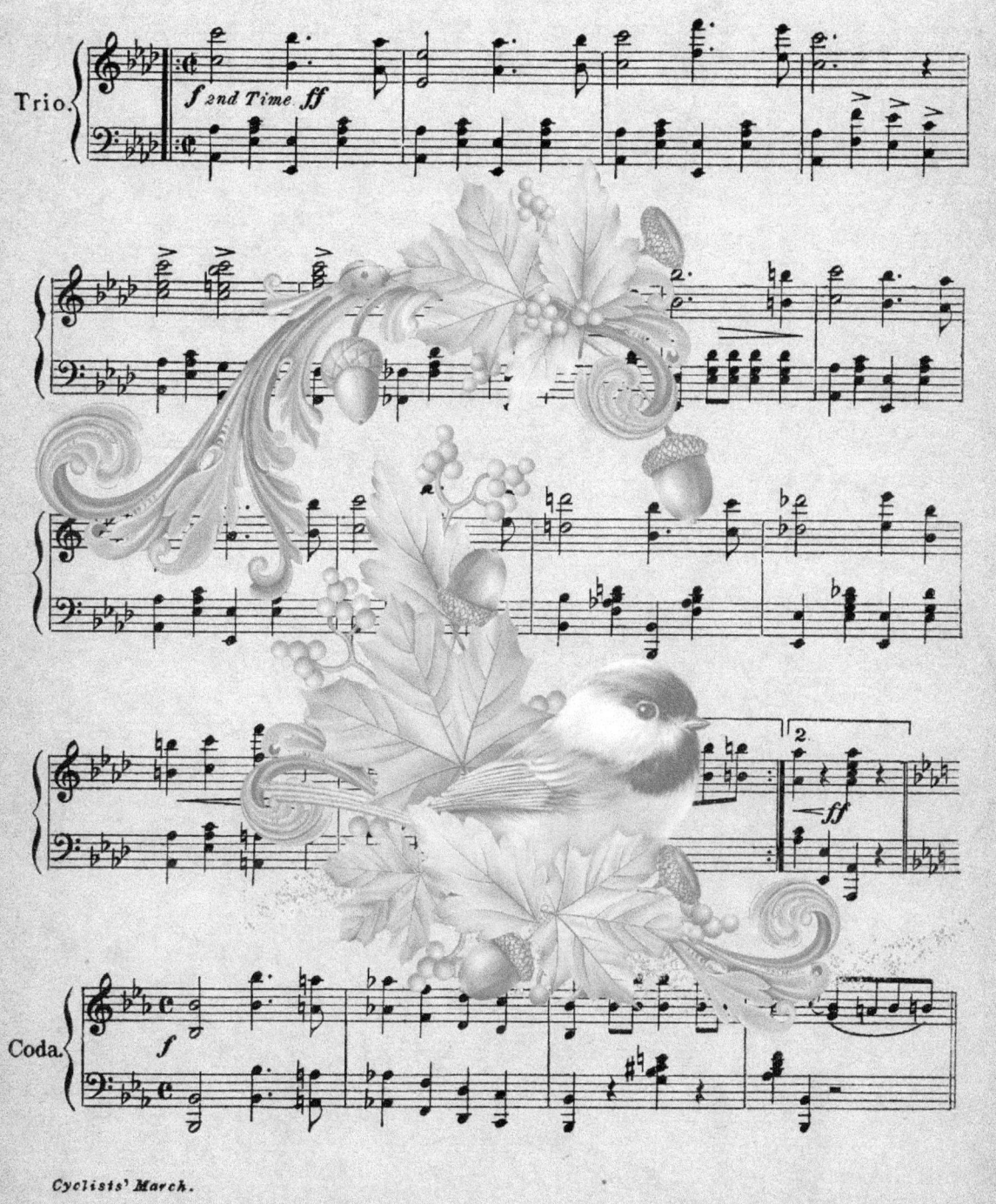

Trio.

f 2nd Time ff

Coda.

f

Cyclists' March.

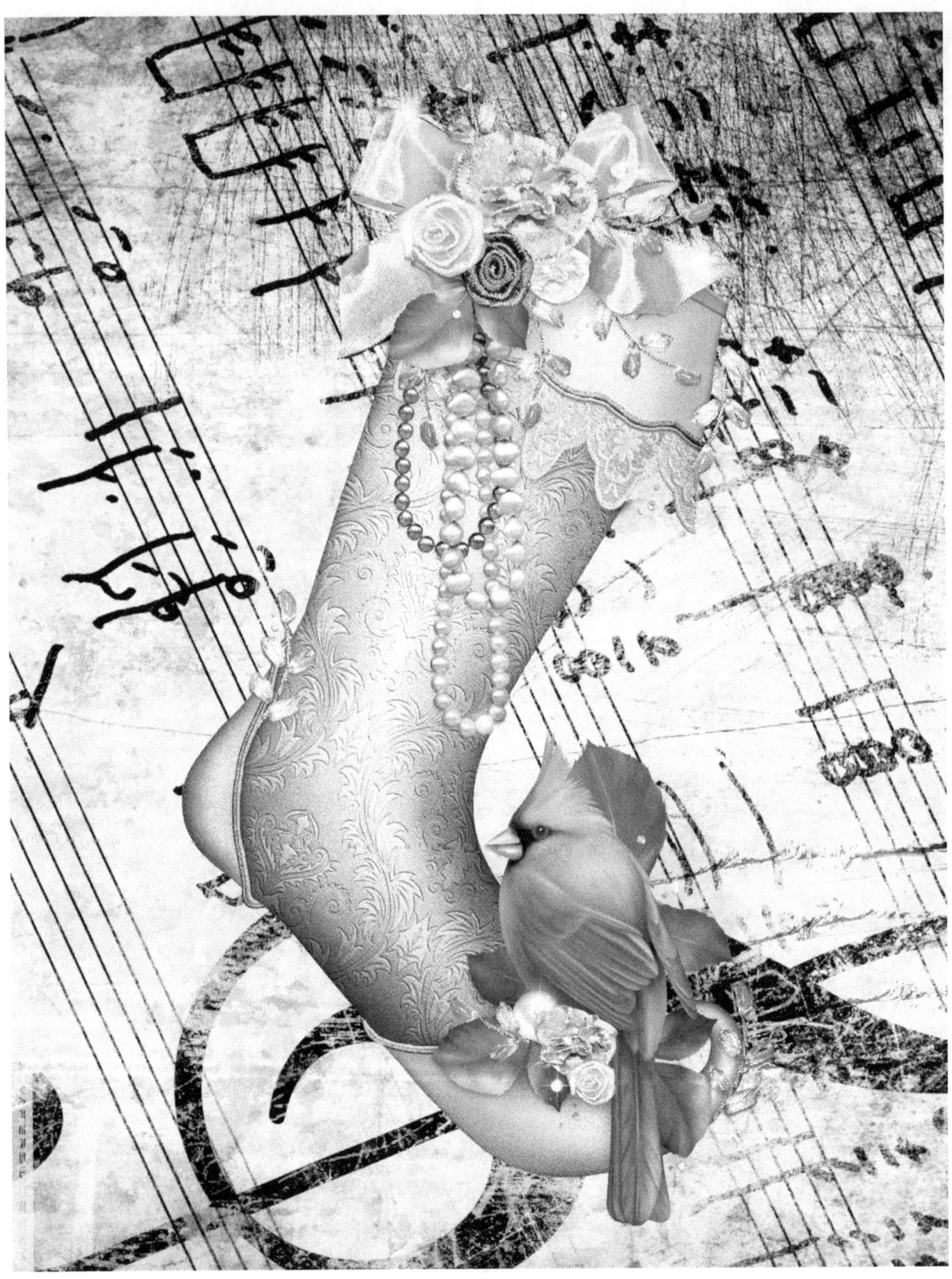

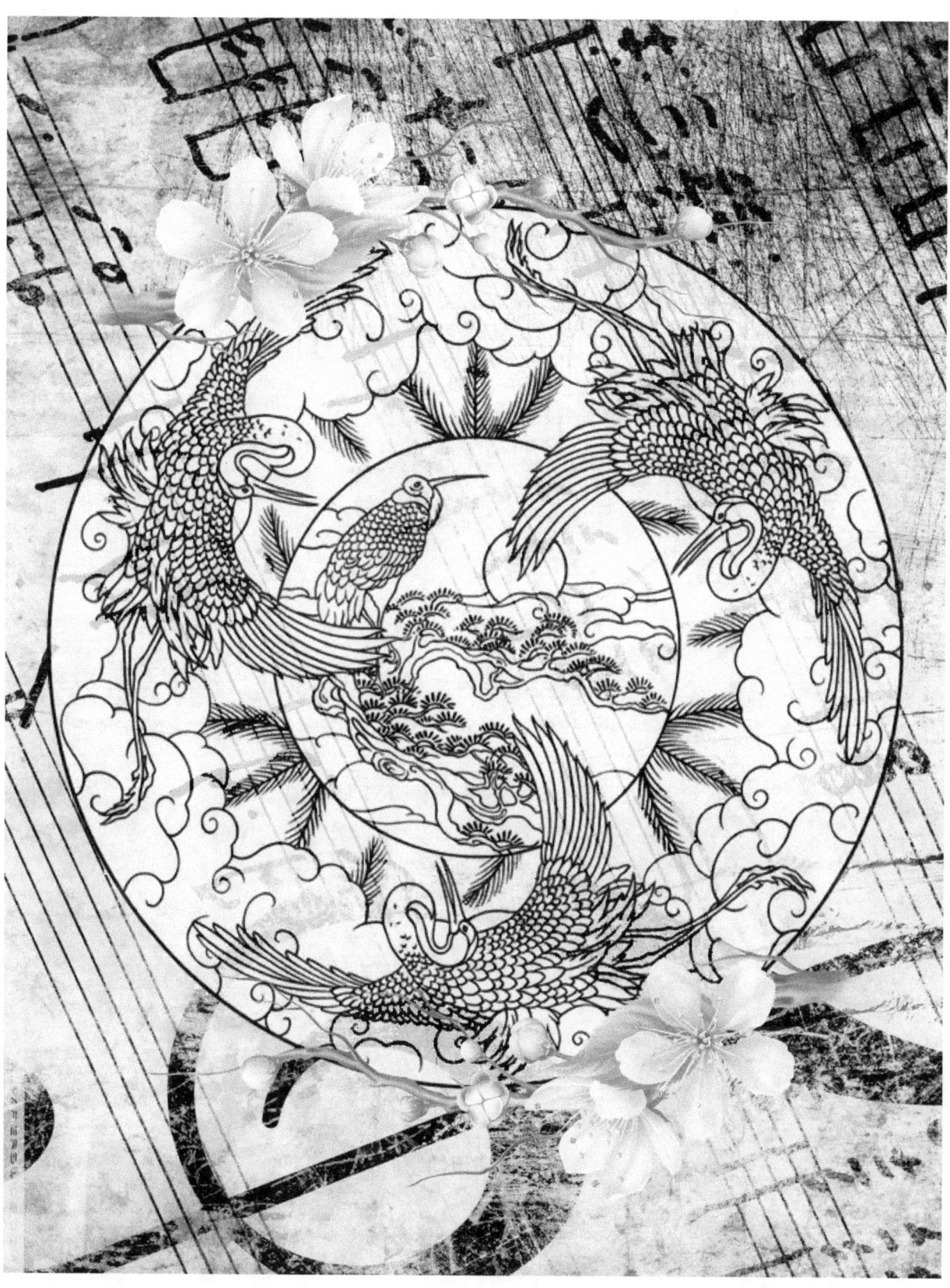

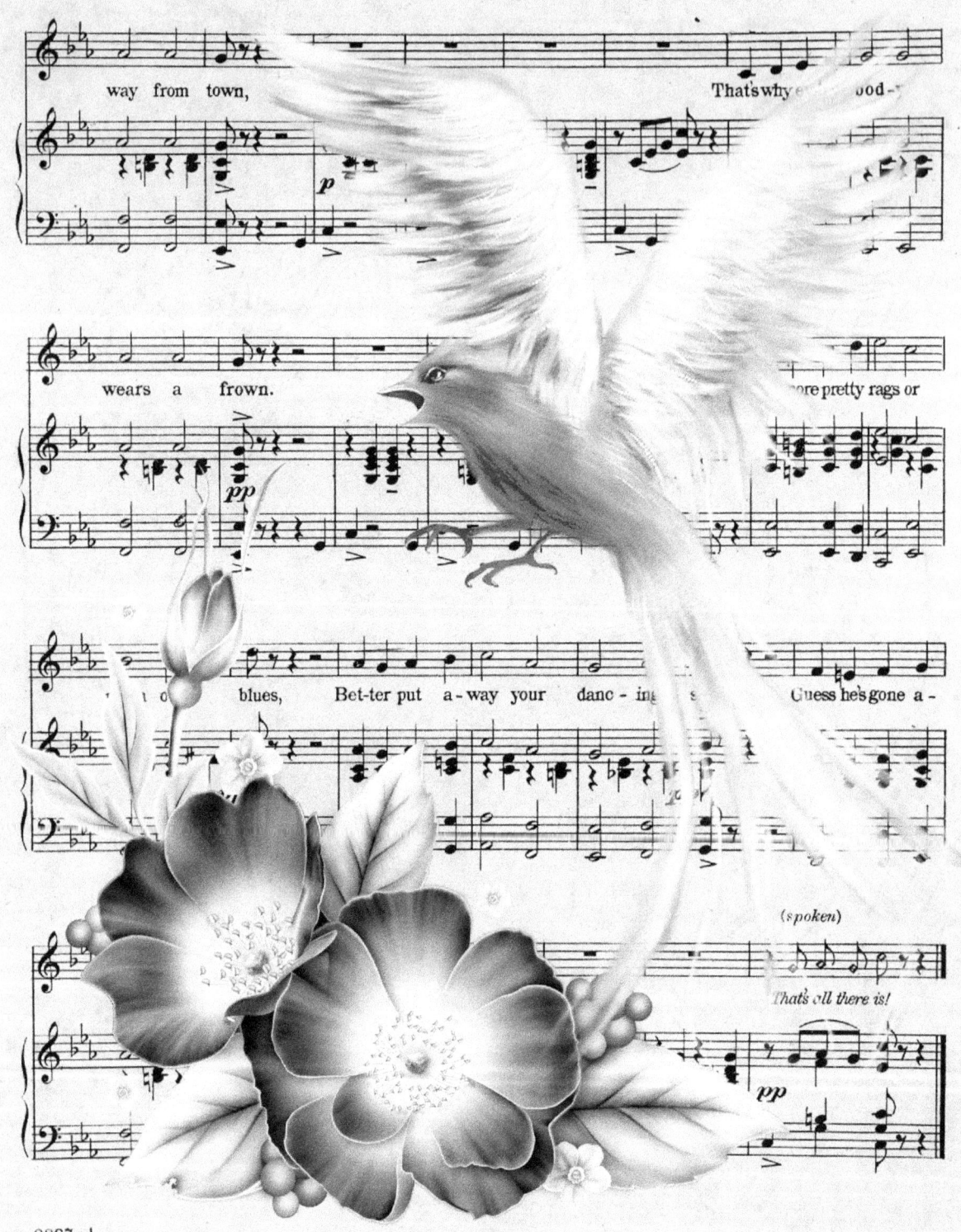

way from town,   That's why e... ...ood-

wears a frown.   ...ore pretty rags or

...blues,   Bet-ter put a-way your danc-ing... ...   Guess he's gone a-

(spoken)

That's all there is!

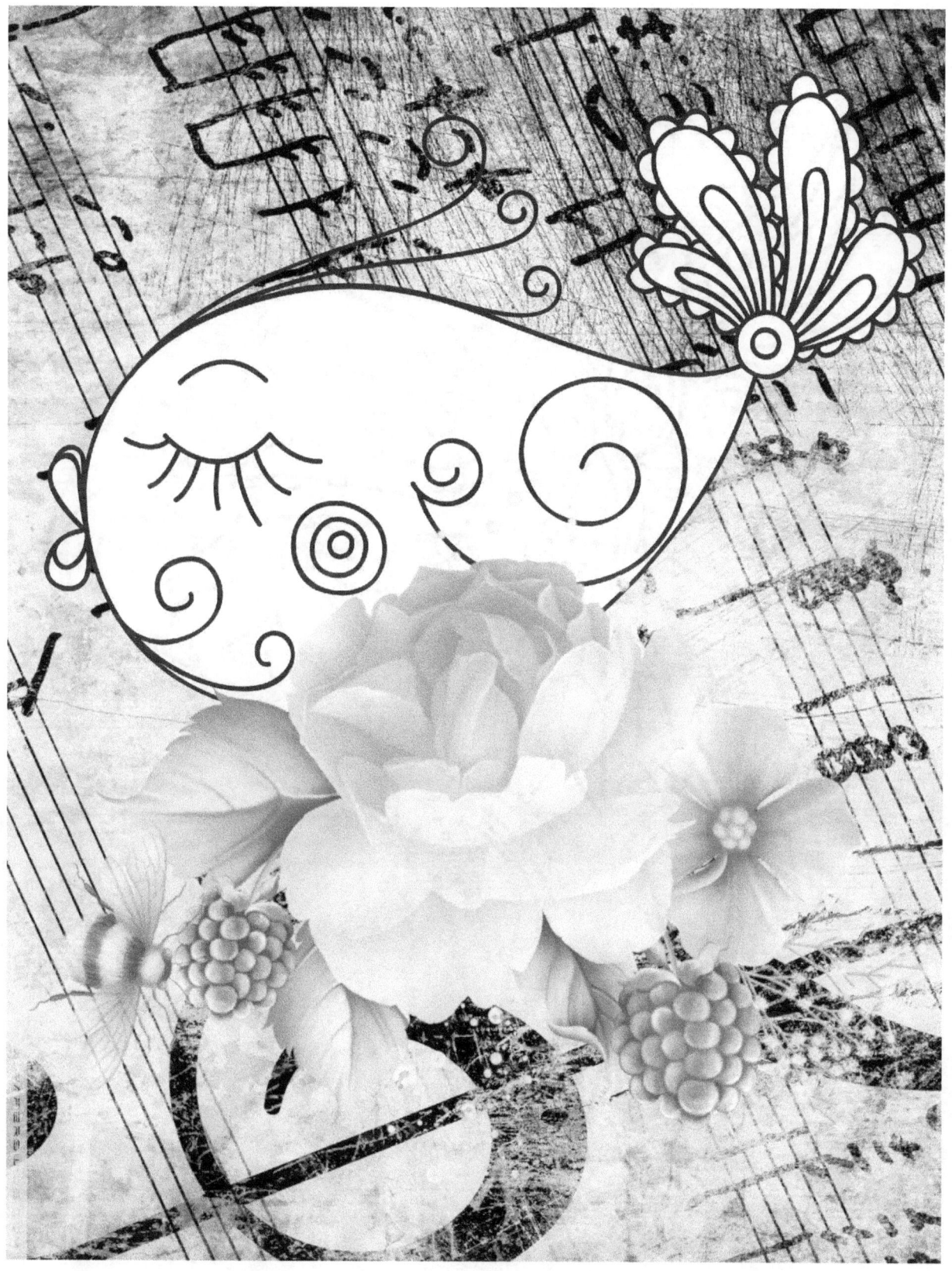

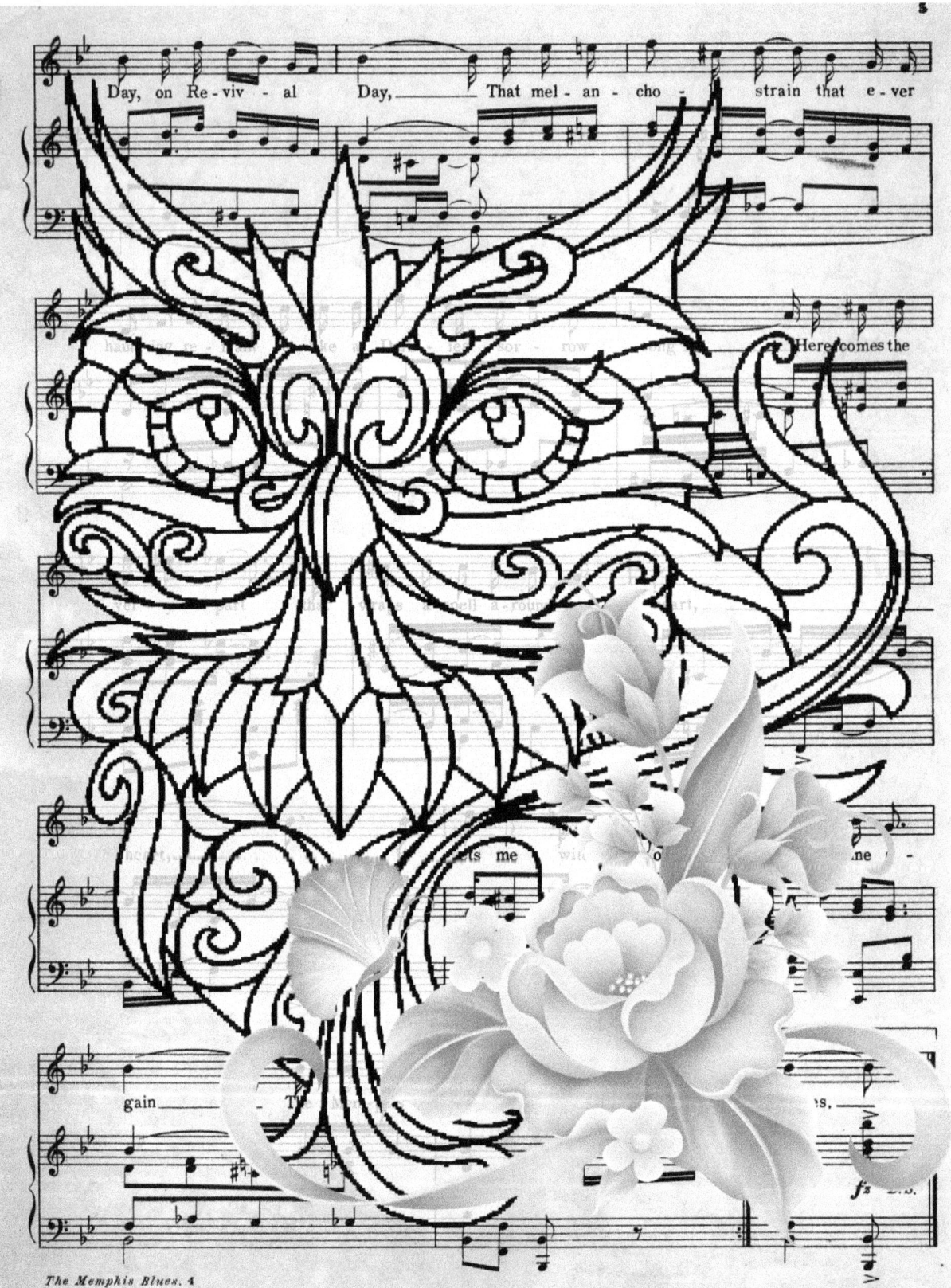

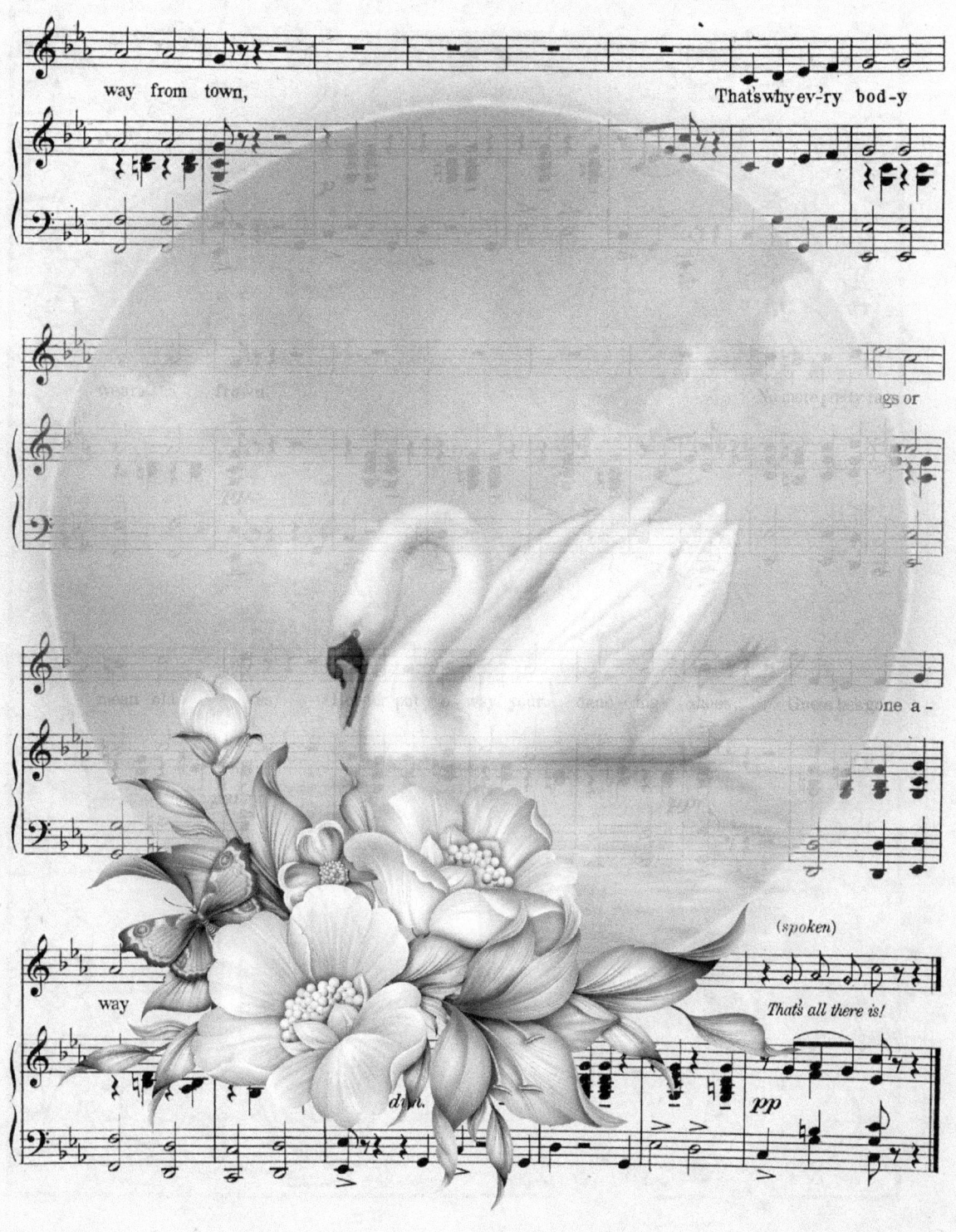

That's why ev'-ry bod-y

No more prettyrags or

Guess he's gone a-

way

(spoken)

That's all there is!

dim.

pp

5

8887-4

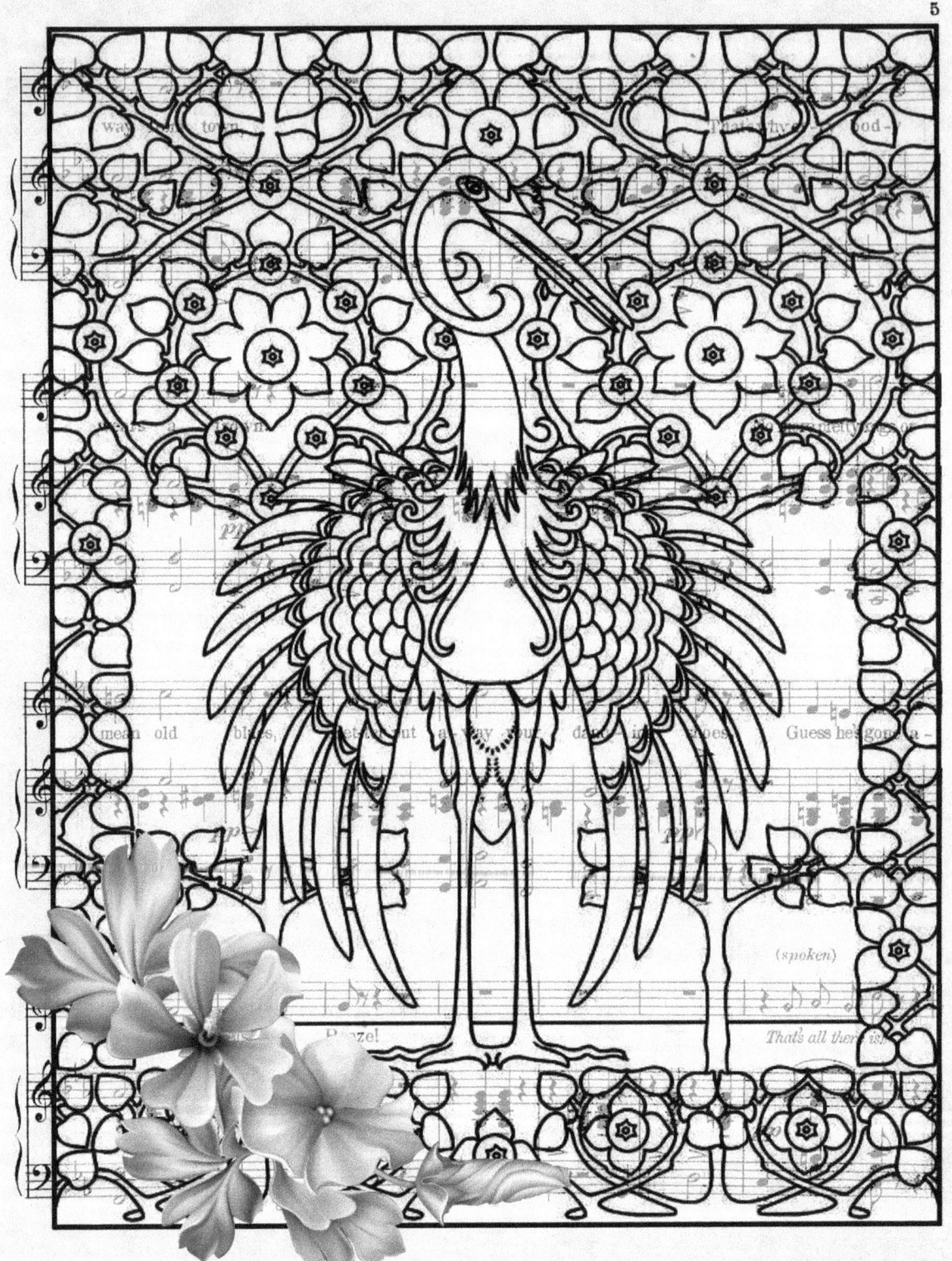